THE
GRACE
COURSE

FROM FREEDOM IN CHRIST MINISTRIES

STEVE GOSS, RICH MILLER
& JUDE GRAHAM

A 6-WEEK DISCIPLESHIP COURSE FOR EVERY CHRISTIAN

LET GOD'S GRACE FREE YOU TO **BE REAL AND BEAR MUCH FRUIT**

Published by Monarch Books
an imprint of
Lion Hudson plc
Wilkinson House, Jordan Hill Road,
Oxford OX2 8DR, England
Email: monarch@lionhudson.com
www.lionhudson.com/monarch

ISBN: 978 0 85721 325 9
ISBN: 978 0 85721 323 5 (pack of five)
E-ISBN: 978 0 85721 268 9

First edition 2012

A catalogue record for this book is available from the British Library

Printed and bound in the UK, September 2012, LH26.

Book Design And Illustrations: Ezekiel Design, Manchester, www.ezekieldesign.co.uk

Contents

Introduction

Why Take Part In *The Grace Course*?

Do you want to keep growing as a Christian, and bear more and more fruit that will last for ever? By God's grace – and only by His grace – you can! The objective of *The Grace Course* is to help you experience God's grace in such a deep way (in your **heart** as well as your head) that love for Him becomes the main motivator in your life. You will learn:

- how to deal with the false motivators of guilt, shame, fear and pride.
- why doing things for God because you feel you have to is worth precisely nothing.
- how to get rid of that "low grade fever" of guilt in your life.
- that you can hold your head up high no matter what's in the past.
- you need fear nothing and no one except God Himself.
- how to deal with sins that grip you.
- why putting others first is always the wise choice.
- that if you want to be really fruitful, it starts with resting.

In short, if you are ready to "do business" with God as you go through this course, our expectation is that you will experience His love like never before so that you can bear more fruit than you ever thought possible!

How To Get The Most Out Of The Course

- Do your best to get to each session and catch up with any you have to miss (perhaps by borrowing the DVDs if available).
- Ensure you take the opportunity to go through *The Steps To Experiencing God's Grace*, a kind and gentle process just between you and God that takes place between Sessions 5 and 6.
- At the end of each session, you will be invited to consider areas where your thinking is not in line with Biblical truth — when you become aware of areas, be sure to write them in the *Lies List* at the back of the book and work out what is actually true from God's Word.
- You will be introduced to "Stronghold-Busting", a straightforward and very effective strategy for renewing your mind (see Romans 12:2) that will help you stand firm in your freedom. Make it part of your daily life.

Bible Translations Used

SESSION 1: FREE!

WELCOME

One definition of grace is "getting what you don't deserve". Tell about a time you got what you didn't deserve. What did you deserve? What did you actually get?

WORSHIP

You belong! See 1 John 3:1.

PRAYER & DECLARATION

Dear Father God, thank You for adopting us as Your children through Jesus Christ, and for giving us the privilege of calling You "Abba, Father"! Please open the eyes of our hearts so that we may really understand what this means for us. Amen.

I have been bought out of slavery by the blood of Jesus. I choose to submit myself to God and I resist anything that would drag me back into slavery.

WORD

Focus verse: 1 Samuel 16:7b: "For the Lord sees not as man sees: man looks on the outward appearance, but the Lord looks on the heart."

Focus truth: In Christ we are perfectly loved and accepted for who we are, not what we do. From that position of security, we can make a free choice to serve God because we love Him, and get rid of any other false motivation.

Introduction

> Through many dangers, toils and snares
> I have already come;
> 'Tis Grace that brought me safe thus far
> and Grace will lead me home.

(*Amazing Grace* by John Newton)

This course is about helping us live in God's grace every moment of every day for the rest of our lives, so that we can become everything God wants us to be and do everything God has for us to do.

In Romans 5:2, Paul tells us that we have obtained by faith "our introduction... into this grace in which we stand" (NASB). But God wants us to go beyond our introduction to grace, He wants us to "grow in the grace and knowledge of our Lord and Saviour Jesus Christ" (2 Peter 3:18).

The objective of the course is to to help you know what it means to experience God's grace every day so that you can be fruitful to the fullest possible extent.

Understanding grace

Jesus said, "If you love me, you will obey my commands" (John 14:15 NCV). How do you hear Him saying it? What expression is on His face?

The story of the two brothers (Luke 15:11–32 NIV)

The younger brother

The younger brother has behaved so badly that he is expecting to be disowned or at best to be severely punished — and that would be what he deserved. Yet his father is looking out for him and runs to meet him, overjoyed to have him back.

The father immediately embraces this smelly, dirty, broken individual, puts rich clothes on him and throws a magnificent party.

He also gives him three things that are laden with symbolism.

The **robe** symbolizes that the son has once again been given the right to enjoy the place of "right standing" with the father, that he is completely restored.

The **ring** symbolizes power and authority to carry out the father's business.

The **sandals** show that the boy, despite everything he has done, is still entitled to the rights of a son.

What is the worst thing you have ever done? If you went out of here and did it again or worse... and then sincerely came back to God, what reception would you get?

The context of the story

The religious people were complaining and saying "This man welcomes sinners and even sits down to eat with them."

Jesus tells this story in response to the accusation that His behaviour was wrong, that it was displeasing to God.

The point of the story is that it is not our behaviour that puts us into a right relationship with God – it's His grace.

But behaviour does matter

Sin has consequences. But one of those consequences was **not** the ending of the son's relationship with his father.

God is rooting for you and has given you everything you need so that you do not have to fail. But if you do, His loving arms are there to welcome you back no matter how badly you have messed up.

Note: there is an old heresy called "antinomianism" which pushes Biblical truth too far and says that, since we are saved by God's grace through faith, there is no need for a moral law so our behaviour doesn't matter. That is not what we are saying as will become clear!

What does "grace" mean to you?

The father gives the younger son three gifts which symbolize things that God has given to you. Which gift is most meaningful to you? Why?

If you knew for sure that God's acceptance of you and love for you did not depend on how well you behaved, how might that change the way you live?

The elder brother — slaving rather than serving

The elder brother is often overlooked but is the character that Jesus was specifically addressing. He did not throw everything back in his father's face. He always toed the line and did what was expected of him so was outraged when his brother was welcomed back with a party after behaving so badly.

He didn't understand that the father's love and acceptance was as little to do with his **good** outward behaviour as it was with the other son's **bad** outward behaviour. It is nothing to do with behaviour. It's all about grace.

He had been "slaving away" day after day for the inheritance he would one day receive. But his father says, "Everything I have is yours". He could have been enjoying everything the Father had for years.

Are we like this brother in that we do not really know what we already have or who we already are?

The story of the labourers in the vineyard (Matthew 20:1–16)

The workers all received the same no matter how long they had been working.

The owner's response was, "Am I not allowed to do what I choose with what belongs to me? Or do you begrudge my generosity?" (Matthew 20:15)

What you receive from God is nothing to do with what you do. It's down to His generosity, His grace.

THE GRACE COURSE | SESSION 1 | FREE!

Are we "slaving" for God?

Both brothers traded in the place of grace and privilege that they had been born into, and chose to walk away from their relationship with his father.

The younger brother found himself "in a distant land" with the pigs. Although the elder brother never left home physically, he is out in the fields "slaving away". He had in effect taken the identity of a hired servant, the identity that the younger son was also expecting to have to take up.

The father's presence alone wasn't enough for the elder son. He preferred to strive for what the father could give him, and was trying to make his father bless him by seeking to do everything right externally, but internally his heart was far away.

Jesus was showing the religious people that if they thought that outward behaviour was enough to earn God's favour, they were terribly deceived.

But what we do is still important

What we do is nevertheless important. At the end of the age, there will be a day when what we have done will be specifically tested by God to see if it has any real value for eternity.

Now if anyone builds on the foundation with gold, silver, precious stones, wood, hay, straw – each one's work will become manifest, for the Day will disclose it, because it will be revealed by fire, and the fire will test what sort of work each one has done. If the work that anyone has built on the foundation survives, he will receive a reward. If anyone's work is burned up, he will suffer loss, though he himself will be saved, but only as through fire.
(1 Corinthians 3:12–15)

Fire will burn up the works that are of no value – "wood, hay, straw" – while works that are of value – "gold, silver, precious stones" – will remain.

Romans 8:1 assures us that there is no **condemnation** for those who are in Christ Jesus but will there be any **commendation**?

Two people can be doing exactly the same thing – feeding the poor perhaps, spending an hour a day reading His word and praying. One will be delighting God, the other not.

It's not what, but why

When God chose David to be King of Israel, Samuel said,

"The Lord sees not as man sees: man looks on the outward appearance, but the Lord looks on the heart." (1 Samuel 16:7b)

What is important to God is not so much **what** we do but **why** we do it. God has never taken pleasure from people just obeying a set of rules outwardly if they are not doing it from the heart.

It's all about our motivation. And if that motivation is not love, then what we do, no matter how good it looks, is worth precisely nothing. It's wood, hay or straw.

In 2 Corinthians 5:14 (NIV), Paul says, "For the love of Christ compels us".

God wants our motivation to be love and nothing but love. But we can easily end up motivated by other things:

- guilt

- shame

- fear

- pride

PAUSE FOR THOUGHT 2

At the end of Jesus' story, the younger brother has been received back as a son but the elder brother continues to act like a slave. How might their attitudes differ towards the work they do for their father?

God wants what we do for Him to be motivated purely by love. What other things can motivate us instead? If you are able, share how you have been motivated by these things.

If we realize that we have been motivated by things other than love, how can we change?

What we do comes from who we are
Consider two pictures:

1. The younger son at the point that he collapses into his father's arms and casts himself on his mercy. He can scarcely believe his father's grace as he realizes that, even though he richly deserves it, he will not be punished. He is forgiven.

2. The same son a matter of minutes later when he is dressed in the finest robe, with the ring on his fingers and the sandals on his feet, feasting on the finest food. He is still acutely aware of his past failures, yet he has been not just forgiven, but completely restored to his position as son with free access to everything his father owns.

Which picture most accurately represents how you see yourself in relation to God?

Whether it feels like it or not, the second picture represents you!

In order to live as the Father wants us to, we have to know that we are more than just forgiven. We are completely restored and deep down inside absolutely acceptable — indeed a delight — to God.

You will get halfway through most of Paul's letters to the churches before you find an instruction on what to do, how to behave. The first half of the letters is all about what has already been done, what you already have, who you now are in Christ. Paul knows that if you grasp that, the rest will flow naturally.

God's love and acceptance of you is nothing to do with your behaviour. But when you stop trying to "act like you think a Christian should act" and just simply live from the truth of who you now are, you'll behave well!

Bondslaves

In New Testament times, it was very common for Roman masters to free their slaves, but sometimes of their own free will they decided to stay and continue to serve in the household simply because of love for the master.

From the outside what they did day-by-day probably didn't look very different but there is in fact a world of difference between doing what you do because you are forced to or, as in the case of the elder brother, to gain some future reward — and doing it simply out of love because you make a free choice.

Paul describes himself as "a slave of Christ" (Romans 1:1).

* We love because He first loved us (1 John 4:19).
* We give freely because we have received freely (Matthew 10:8b).
* We are merciful because He has been merciful to us (Luke 6:36).
* We forgive because we have been forgiven (Ephesians 4:32).

God the Father — looking for relationship

At the start of our experience of Jesus, we know we're the younger son. We know we need Him.

At that point we're meant to go on a journey to becoming like the Father but most of us in fact end up going on a journey to become like the elder brother, slaving away for God.

You have a great master! He has some significant works that He has prepared in advance for you to do. But He doesn't force you in any way to do them. He will love you whatever you do. However, as you make a choice to serve Him just because you love Him, you'll find it becomes a real pleasure to do the work He gives you to do!

Uncovering faulty thinking

Use the *Lies List* on the last two pages of this book to note down any areas where you realize that your belief system is not quite in line with what God tells us is really true. Note the "lies" down on the left hand side and, if you can, try to find corresponding truths to write on the right hand side.

This session may have highlighted lies such as:
- what I have done is too bad for God to forgive me or to accept me back.
- God loves other people but He can't really love me.
- I have to live up to a certain set of standards for God to be pleased with me.
- God loves me more when I work hard for Him.

WITNESS

People who don't yet know God as their Father are like spiritual orphans. What do orphans need? How can I help meet that need?

IN THE COMING WEEK

The story of the two sons turns on the character of the father who, of course, represents God. He is not an inspecting sergeant-major figure looking for us to put a foot wrong. Jesus portrays a father who longs to fellowship with his sons. He runs to meet the younger son. He goes out to plead with the older son.

Sometimes our earthly fathers have not been all they might have been. Maybe we never knew our father. This makes it difficult to know God as the perfect Father He is because we tend to project our experiences onto Him. Use the My Father God statements overleaf every day this week (and for as long as it takes after that) to renounce lies that you may believe and joyfully affirm what is really true about Him.

I renounce the lie that my Father God is:	I joyfully accept the truth that my Father God is:
distant and uninterested in me.	intimate and involved (see Psalm 139:1–18).
insensitive and uncaring.	kind and compassionate (see Psalm 103:8–14).
stern and demanding.	accepting and filled with joy and love (see Romans 15:7; Zephaniah 3:17).
passive and cold.	warm and affectionate (see Isaiah 40:11; Hosea 11:3–4).
absent or too busy for me.	always with me and eager to be with me (see Hebrews 13:5; Jeremiah 31:20; Ezekiel 34:11–16).
impatient, angry or never satisfied with what I do.	patient and slow to anger and delights in those who put their hope in His unfailing love (see Exodus 34:6; 2 Peter 3:9, Psalm 147:11).
mean, cruel or abusive.	loving and gentle and protective (see Jeremiah 31:3; Isaiah 42:3; Psalm 18:2).

I renounce the lie that my Father God is:	I joyfully accept the truth that my Father God is:
trying to take all the fun out of life.	trustworthy and wants to give me a full life; His will is good, perfect and acceptable for me (see Lamentations 3:22–23; John 10:10; Romans 12:1,2).
controlling or manipulative.	full of grace and mercy, and gives me freedom to fail (see Hebrews 4:15–16; Luke 15:11–16).
condemning or unforgiving.	tender-hearted and forgiving; His heart and arms are always open to me (see Psalm 130:1–4; Luke 15:17–24).
nit-picking or a demanding perfectionist.	committed to my growth and proud of me as His growing child (see Romans 8:28–29; Hebrews 12:5–11; 2 Corinthians 7:14).

I am the Apple of His Eye!

SESSION 2: INNOCENT!

WELCOME

Which road sign would best describe where you are on your journey with God right now? (eg, stop, steep gradient, diversion/detour, crossroads)

WORSHIP

Thank You for the cross! See John 14:6.

PRAYER & DECLARATION

Father, by Your Spirit, please show us life-changing truths that will set us free to experience Your gift of life in all its fullness. Amen.

In Christ, I am forgiven and declared innocent of all the charges that were stacked against me. So by the authority of the Lord Jesus Christ I command any accusing and condemning thoughts in my mind to go now.

WORD

Focus verse: When you were dead in your transgressions and the uncircumcision of your flesh, He made you alive together with Him, having forgiven us all our transgressions, having cancelled out the certificate of debt consisting of decrees against us, which was hostile to us; and He has taken it out of the way, having nailed it to the cross. (Colossians 2:13–14 NASB)

Focus truth: No matter what we have done (even as Christians) and no matter how guilty we may feel, the truth is that our guilt has been completely and utterly paid for by Christ's death on the cross so that we can stand confidently before God, who is pure and holy.

Introduction

Many of us walk around with the sense that we are failing miserably as sons and daughters of God.

Carrying a load of guilt makes us like the elder brother: our motivation to do good and avoid sin is so that we will somehow gain or maintain God's love rather than first resting in the unconditional love of God and being motivated by love.

What is guilt?

True guilt has nothing to do with feelings. It's about hard facts.

Guilt is a legal term, used when a judge or jury pronounces a defendant guilty.

Guilt is defined in relation to the legal authority which has laid down the laws. If we break the laws of that legal authority we are guilty. If we do not, we are innocent.

True guilt and guilt feelings are not the same thing.

Are you guilty?

We may well be law-abiding citizens, innocent before the laws of the land. But where do we stand before the heavenly Judge?

God's holiness

God's holiness is such that it would be impossible for Him to tolerate sin, to gloss over it, to say it didn't matter. He wouldn't be God if He did.

God chose to give us free will. So our ancestor, Adam, was created perfect and innocent, yet with the capacity to choose good or evil.

The consequences of sin

Adam chose to disobey God, and that disobedience is what the Bible calls sin.

"The wages of sin is death". (Romans 6:23)

Adam incurred true guilt before God because he had broken God's law.

In many languages the words "sin" and "debt" are the same.

If you are found guilty before a human court, payment is usually demanded either in the form of a financial penalty (a fine), or time that you have to serve in prison. Once that debt is paid, you are again declared free. You have paid your dues or served your time.

Paul says, "by the one man's disobedience the many were made sinners" (Romans 5:19). When Adam sinned, one of the consequences is that you and I and all his descendants were made guilty before God too.

There are three ways guilt can come. First, by our natural bent for evil passed down from Adam. Second by outright rebellion against God, and third by missing the mark when we try to do good.

Share with the group what the word "debt" brings to mind. Have you ever had a debt you couldn't pay?

What happened that caused us to begin our lives owing God a huge debt we couldn't pay? How do you feel about that?

Can you think of an example of a time when you or someone else did something wrong, but did not feel guilty, or conversely felt guilty for something that wasn't actually wrong?

Getting rid of guilt

In Roman times, if someone was found guilty of breaking the law and sent to prison, an itemized list was made of everything they had done wrong and the corresponding time they had to serve in order to pay the debt. It was called a "Certificate of Debt" and was nailed to the cell door.

Every single person who came after Adam was born with a Certificate of Debt to God. As we grow up, we gradually become aware of a sense of guilt, which we try to get rid of.

Strategies to get rid of guilt that don't work

Justification by good works

This, the most popular strategy, is where we try, in effect, to prove our innocence before God by doing good things: keeping the commandments; reading the Bible; attending church regularly; giving money to the church or to the poor; feeding the hungry; and so on.

Now, all these good works (often referred to in the Bible as "works of the Law") are good but they do not balance the measuring scale of our lives. There is no set of scales where the good deeds are weighed against evil to see if we get to Heaven. "A person is not justified by the works of the law... because by the works of the law no one will be justified. (Galatians 2:16)

A test!

- Are you filled with a sense of God's eagerness to bless you, confident of His love for you only when you feel you are doing **well** as a Christian?
- What happens when you fail to do the things on your spiritual "To Do" list or mess up and do something on your spiritual "To Don't" list? Do those feelings change?
- Are you plagued by a vague, nagging, gnawing sense that God is distant and somehow disapproving of you?
- Do you tend to make a vow to yourself or to God that "I'll do better tomorrow" and determine to work twice as hard the next day to please Him?

Justification by religious background

This is thinking that God will accept you because of your religious background or upbringing.

The apostle Paul admitted that he once put his trust in his religious background:

> If anyone else has a mind to put confidence in the flesh, I far more; circumcised the eighth day, of the nation of Israel, of the tribe of Benjamin, a Hebrew of Hebrews, as to the Law, a Pharisee; as to zeal, a persecutor of the church; as to the righteousness which is in the Law, found blameless. (Philippians 3:4–6 NASB)

But our religious backgrounds mean nothing to God apart from Christ, and they have no power to remove our guilt. Paul came to realize, "but whatever things were gain to me, those things I have counted as loss for the sake of Christ" (Philippians 3:7 NASB). In fact he goes on to call them "rubbish".

Justification by comparison

This is where we think thoughts like, "Well, at least I don't _____ like so and so." And we fill in the blank with some kind of sin that we deem worse than anything we have ever done, and feel better about ourselves.

See Luke 18:9–14 for what Jesus said about this.

God's remedy for guilt

You may be struggling with the concept that one man could represent us all and make us all guilty, but thankfully it worked both ways:

> And just as all people were made sinners as the result of the disobedience of one man, in the same way they will be put right with God as the result of the obedience of the one man. (Romans 5:17 GNT)

We were all born with a Certificate of Debt, but Colossians 2:13–14 says it was cancelled by being nailed to the cross with Christ.

When the Roman prisoner had served out the full time allotted, when he had paid his debt to society, he was released. A judge would take the yellowed, tattered Certificate of Debt and write "Paid In Full" across it. Having paid the debt he once again became "not guilty" of those crimes.

Just before Jesus died on the cross, He let out a loud victorious shout (see Matthew 27:50) which is usually translated "It is finished" (John 19:30). The word that Jesus used is the exact same word that the Roman judge wrote across the released criminal's Certificate of Debt: "Paid In Full!"

This declaration of "not guilty" is not just for when we first came to Christ. God's grace is for every moment of every day. For those in Christ Jesus, no sin we commit can ever take away one bit from the full and complete sacrifice Jesus paid for us. Despite our sin, we are still forgiven. Our guilt is still gone. Forever.

Simon and the sinful woman (Luke 7:36–50)

Simon was confident in his religious background and all the good things he did. He saw himself as a fine, upstanding member of society. He didn't realize his guilt before God. He certainly didn't feel guilty.

The woman on the other hand knew that she was guilty yet Jesus declared that she was forgiven even though she was a prostitute.

So how is it that a law-abiding man of good standing remains guilty before God whilst a lady who had been up to that point engaged in what many would see as the ultimate sinful life is declared innocent?

Jesus told her that her faith had saved her.

> For by grace you have been saved through faith. And this is not your own doing; it is the gift of God. (Ephesians 2:8)

Being declared not guilty is a pure grace gift from God. It is activated by faith. What does that look like? Simply turning to Him in sheer desperation and asking Him for salvation.

PAUSE FOR THOUGHT 2

We're going to ask God to reveal to us all of the false expectations and standards that we have felt we have to live up to and which have become a burden to us or made us feel like failures. Pray together:

Loving Father,

I thank You that in Christ all of Your expectations of me have been fully met, (Romans 8:4) and that You have forgiven me all my transgressions and cancelled out my certificate of debt by nailing it to the cross (Colossians 2:13–14). I confess that I have believed the lie that I have needed something more than Christ in order to gain or maintain acceptance with You and others. Please would You reveal to me now all the expectations, standards and demands that I have been living under, by which I have sought to become more acceptable and feel less guilty, so that I can return in simple faith to relying just on Christ's work on my behalf. I ask this in the name of Jesus Christ, who died for me. Amen.

Then spend time just between you and God writing down the false expectations He shows you on a separate sheet. Consider the following:

- expectations you wrongly believed were from God
- expectations from parents and family
- expectations from teachers
- expectations from churches and church leaders
- expectations from employers
- other false expectations

Then for each false expectation that you have listed, say the following:

I renounce the lie that I have to live up to the expectation of:
_____ in order to feel good enough, valued or accepted. Thank You, Lord Jesus, that in You I meet all of God's expectations and that nothing I could do could make You love me more or love me less. Amen.

Finally, tear up the list you made and move on!

Shouldn't the father in the story of the two sons have been portrayed as at least a little angry? Wasn't the way he so quickly forgave his son and restored him to the family a bit premature? Would it not have been better to make the son feel guilty about what he did? Isn't guilt a very effective deterrent to sin?

When Paul had to rebuke the Corinthian church, he wrote:

I … rejoice, not because you were grieved, but because you were grieved into repenting; … For you felt a godly grief, so that you suffered no loss through us. For godly grief produces a repentance that leads to salvation without regret, whereas worldly grief produces death.
(2 Corinthians 7:9–10)

Paul did not want the Corinthians to feel guilt. What he wanted them to feel was godly grief (or sorrow) which, he says, produces a repentance without regret.

Guilt feelings tend to make us want to run away from God rather than come to Him in repentance without regret. Guilt feelings seem more like what Paul calls "worldly" sorrow which produces death.

Grace, not guilt, is the most powerful motivator to keep us from sinning. Why? Because guilt drives us away from God whereas grace draws us close to Him — and that's where the only real protection from sin can be found.

For the grace of God has appeared, bringing salvation for all people, training us to renounce all ungodliness and worldly passions, and to live self-controlled, upright, and godly lives, in the present age (Titus 2:11–12).

When we sin

God wants your sense of sorrow not to drive you away from Him but to drive you into His arms, where you will find the same welcome the younger son received. Then you can confess your sins, accept His forgiveness and turn away from them.

This restores our intimacy with Christ and we experience a cleansing of our spirit, soul and body from sin's corruption. And no regret.

"But what if I still feel guilty after doing all that?"

Then your feelings are lying to you. Focus on the truth. You are forgiven!

Three helpful pictures

"Come now, let us reason together," says the Lord. "Though your sins are like scarlet, they shall be as white as snow; though they are red like crimson, they shall become like wool". (Isaiah 1:18)

You will again have compassion on us; you will tread our sins underfoot and hurl all our iniquities into the depths of the sea. (Micah 7:19 NIV)

A truth to remember

There is therefore now no condemnation for those who are in Christ Jesus. (Romans 8:1)

That is not just religious talk or wishful thinking; it is the truth about you!

Remember what Jesus says to you: "Your sins are forgiven... Your faith has saved you; go in peace."

PAUSE FOR THOUGHT 3

Which of the pictures of how God has dealt with our sin means most to you? Why?

Uncovering faulty thinking

Use the *Lies List* on the last two pages of this book to note down any areas where you realize that you have not been believing what is actually true according to God's Word.

This session may have highlighted lies such as:

- I am only forgiven if I confess my sins really hard and cry tears over them.
- Feeling guilty for my sins is the best safeguard against doing them again.
- My sins are too big to be forgiven.
- Guilt is a good way to motivate others to do right.

 **WITNESS**

How would you explain to someone with no Christian background why we all need to be declared "Innocent!" by God?

 **IN THE COMING WEEK**

Choose one of the verses that speak about the full extent of God's unconditional love and forgiveness, and commit to declare it out loud with faith for the next 40 days.

"Come now, let us reason together," says the Lord. "Though your sins are like scarlet, they shall be as white as snow; though they are red like crimson, they shall become like wool." (Isaiah 1:18)

You will again have compassion on us; you will tread our sins underfoot and hurl all our iniquities into the depths of the sea. (Micah 7:19 NIV)

Who is a God like you, who pardons sin and forgives the transgression of the remnant of his inheritance? You do not stay angry forever but delight to show mercy. (Micah 7:18 NIV)

SESSION 3: **UNASHAMED!**

WELCOME
Tell the group about an embarrassing moment you have experienced.

WORSHIP
We are welcome in God's presence. (Hebrews 4:16, Hebrews 10:19–22)

PRAYER & DECLARATION
Dear Father, You are holy, pure and without fault, and I confess that there are times when I feel dirty and not good enough to be in Your presence. But I choose to believe the truth that You have made me completely clean and brand new. Please heal any wounds in my heart that would keep me distant from You. Thank You. In the Holy name of Jesus. Amen.

I declare the truth that I am now a new creation in Christ; the old has gone and the new has come! I have been cleansed from sin and no longer have to hide behind masks. I command every enemy of the Lord Jesus to leave my presence.

WORD
Focus verse: For our sake he made him to be sin who knew no sin, so that in him we might become the righteousness of God. (2 Corinthians 5:21)

Focus truth: We have not just been covered with the righteousness of Christ. We have actually **become** the righteousness of God.

The origin of shame

Shame has been around since the Garden of Eden. Adam and Eve did something spectacularly wrong. You'd expect them to feel guilty but it's not obvious that they did.

Before Adam sinned, "The man and his wife were both naked and they felt no shame." (Genesis 2:25 NIV)

After the fall, "The eyes of both were opened, and they knew that they were naked. And they sewed fig leaves together and made themselves loincloths." (Genesis 3:7)

What they immediately felt was somehow deeper than guilt, more fundamental. It was not so much guilt as shame.

The English word "shame" originally meant "covering up".

What is shame?

Guilt says, "I did something wrong. I made a mistake."

Shame says, "There's something wrong with me. I **am** the mistake."

Shame is the painful emotional experience that comes from believing that there is something very wrong, not so much with what we have **done** but with who we **are**.

Where does shame come from?

Being brought up in a shame-based culture

Western societies tend to use guilt to persuade people to conform.

Eastern societies tend to use shame to persuade people to conform.

In a shame-based society, control is maintained by creating a sense that, if you do not conform to social norms, you yourself are not acceptable. Living up to the image of what is socially acceptable becomes the main cultural value. The fear of being rejected and ostracized is a powerful motivator.

Some families and religious institutions can create mini shame-based cultures even in a guilt-based society. A church leader or parent may overuse the words "ought to" and "should" to make you feel that you have to behave in a certain way to be an accepted part of the church or family or to be a "good Christian". They broadcast shame messages like: You should be ashamed of yourself!; You're a disgrace to the family or church!; Why can't you be more like your brother (sister)?; You'll never amount to anything!; I wish you'd never been born!

Things we have done

Any sin that degrades our bodies or causes others to look down on us is a source of shame.

Things others have done to us

Too often the victim rather than the one truly responsible is the one that experiences the shame.

Jesus came specifically to bind up broken hearts and set you free.

Believing wrong messages

If we believe the world's lies that we have to be beautiful or slim or whatever to fit in, we can feel tremendous shame if we think we don't measure up.

When the younger son said, "I am no longer worthy to be called your son," he was experiencing shame that struck at his very identity. "Make me as one of your hired servants." He was ready to exchange his son-identity for that of a servant who would be accepted only on the basis of performance.

Shame's basic message is that we're not good enough. Not good enough for others to value us and not good enough to be God's children. It tells us that the best we can hope for is to slave away in the hope that we might one day become acceptable.

Shame drives us to cover up and hide.

Ways we try to cover up and hide

Some of the more common strategies we can develop to cover up and hide include:

- lying about your accomplishments (or lack) or things in your past you're ashamed of.
- pretending that everything is okay and that you are doing great when you know you're not.
- blame-shifting by making everyone else appear to be the problem rather than you.
- compromising moral or biblical values to fit in, so as to avoid the shame of rejection.
- compensating for shameful deficiencies in one area by seeking to excel in others.
- moralizing by preaching hard against ways that you yourself have behaved and are ashamed of.
- criticizing others harshly in order to make them appear inferior to you
- self-medicating in order to blunt the sting and numb the pain of your own shame.
- striving for perfection in your behaviour or your looks to compensate for the painful belief that you fall far short of who you believe you should be.

But like Adam and Eve's fig leaves, these defence mechanisms don't work. They may provide temporary relief, even convincing us for a time that we

are safe. But in the end, like all strategies of the flesh, they fail. God's way to remove disgrace is grace.

God's remedy for shame

Shame says that we are what is wrong and puts us into "the less mess". We believe that we are "less" than others. We feel helpless, worthless, meaningless, powerless, hopeless. It strikes at our belief about who we are, our identity.

God's remedy is to give us a new identity.

Our old identity

We were (past tense) at one time "by nature children of wrath" (Ephesians 2:3). Our heart, the very core of our being, was "deceitful above all things, and desperately sick" (Jeremiah 17:9).

The great exchange

For our sake he made him to **be** sin who knew no sin, so that in him we might **become** the righteousness of God. (2 Corinthians 5:21)

Jesus did not die just to pay the penalty of your sin. He took on Himself your defiled, unclean nature and destroyed your inner contamination. In exchange you became someone very different to who you were before. You became the righteousness of God. Your heart is no longer deceitful and beyond cure. That great prophecy of Ezekiel was fulfilled that we would have a new heart and a new spirit (Ezekiel 11:19).

We are no longer by nature objects of wrath. Peter tells us that now we actually share God's divine nature (2 Peter 1:4). Our shame has been completely taken away. Once and for all. Past, present and future!

Our new identity

> Therefore, if anyone is in Christ, he is a new creation. The old has passed
> away; behold, the new has come. (2 Corinthians 5:17)

Two thousand years ago, you and I and all those who are in Christ died on
the cross with Christ. Our old sin-loving, shameful self was killed. Dead.
Gone. A biologist might translate 2 Corinthians 5:17, "If anyone is in Christ,
he is a new species"!

Feelings of shame make us want to **draw back** from a holy, righteous God.
But we don't have to run away any more. We don't have to hide. No matter
what is in our past. Because we have a totally new, clean identity in Christ.

You are invited to **draw near** in full assurance and enter a deep relationship
with God Himself in the Holy of Holies because you have been cleansed and
made holy in the deepest part of your being! See Hebrews 10:19–22.

**Are you going to believe what God's Word says about you? Or are you
going to believe what your past experiences tell you?**

A new name

> The nations shall see your righteousness, and all the kings your glory,
> And you shall be called by a new name that the mouth of the Lord will
> give.
> You shall be a crown of beauty in the hand of the Lord, and a royal diadem
> in the hand of your God,
> You shall no more be termed Forsaken, and your land shall no more be
> termed Desolate,
> But you shall be called My Delight Is In Her, and your land Married.
> (Isaiah 62:2–4)

PAUSE FOR THOUGHT 2

Which one of your "new names" particularly strikes a chord with you?

What could you do to make this truth real in your life?

How might knowing this truth in your heart rather than just your head affect how you relate to God and to others?

Planned **Clean**
Loved Unashamed
Treasured **Protected**

Staying free of sin

One of the implications of our new, fresh, clean, shame-free life is that we can keep it fresh, clean and shame-free, and do not have to keep returning to the same old cycles of sin that otherwise keep us trapped in shame. Your new identity is the key to knowing freedom from sin:

> We know that our old self was crucified with him in order that the body of sin might be brought to nothing, so that we would no longer be enslaved to sin. For one who has died has been set free from sin. (Romans 6:6–7)

Paul's is saying that, if death no longer has dominion over you, then neither does sin. This is all about understanding the implications of our new identity. He is at pains to help us realize that our old self that used to live independently of God has been put to death with Christ. And that means we don't any longer have to dance to sin's tune.

Realize you are now dead to sin

> So you also should consider yourselves to be dead to the power of sin and alive to God through Christ Jesus. Do not let sin control the way you live; do not give in to sinful desires. Do not let any part of your body become an instrument of evil to serve sin. Instead, give yourselves completely to God, for you were dead, but now you have new life. So use your whole body as an instrument to do what is right for the glory of God. Sin is no longer your master, for you no longer live under the requirements of the law. Instead, you live under the freedom of God's grace. (Romans 6:11–14 NLT)

First we are to consider ourselves "dead to sin" because we are dead to sin, ie we are no longer in a slave — master relationship with sin. Then we are to make a choice not to surrender the parts of our body to sin, but instead to give our body and all its parts to God... for doing right.

Recognize the reality of the devil and resist him

Even though we acknowledge the reality of the devil and demons intellectually and theologically, those of us brought up in the West are predisposed to ignore the reality of the spiritual world when it comes to living our daily lives and exercising our ministries. The Bible tells us that when we sin, we give the devil a foothold, a point of influence in our lives.

It's all very well receiving forgiveness for your sin, but you're still walking around with a foothold of the enemy in your life. And that unresolved sin will short-circuit God's power to enable you to live righteously. It makes it difficult to resist further temptation and difficult to make the right choice. And the more you seem unable to get out of the cycle, the more the enemy accuses you and the more shame you feel. At this point so many give up and walk away.

Just sinning and confessing, sinning and confessing, doesn't do it. Why? Because that's not complete repentance.

James 4:7 says, "Submit... to God. Resist the devil, and he will flee from you." Confessing is just the first bit — the submitting. We need to go on and complete our responsibility by actively resisting the devil and taking back the foothold that we've given to him that allows sin to reign in our body.

Renew your mind

Then we can go on to renew our minds which is where the transformation comes. It's about replacing the lies we've been believing with truth.

PAUSE FOR THOUGHT 3

What effect does it have on us, and those we are in relationship with, when we try to keep things hidden because we feel ashamed?

When we have fallen into sin, what are the steps we can take to enable us to recover from it?

How will considering yourself "dead to sin" change the way you respond the next time you are tempted to sin?

Truth & lies

Ask God to show you areas where your thinking is not in line with truth and note them down in the *Lies List* at the back of the book. They may be along the lines that:

* something in the past will always affect your identity
* something that was done to you makes you inherently dirty when God says you are clean
* you are somehow "less" than others
* you can't get out of a sin you have been caught in

 WITNESS

How would you share your new name with a non-Christian friend and explain what it means to you?

 IN THE COMING WEEK

Look up the Bible references in the *My New Name* list (on the next page). Tell one or more people who were not at the session about your new name.

If you are caught in a cycle of sin — confess, sin — confess where you keep returning to the same old sin, use the exercise on page 50.

My New Name

My new name is Beloved (Colossians 3:12)

My new name is Beautiful (Psalm 149:4, Song of Songs 4:1)

My new name is Chosen (Ephesians 1:4)

My new name is Precious (Isaiah 43:4)

My new name is Safe (1 John 5:18)

My new name is Loved (1 John 4:10)

My new name is Clean (John 15:3)

My new name is Presentable (Hebrews 10:22)

My new name is Protected (Psalm 91:14, John 17:15)

My new name is Welcomed (Ephesians 3:12)

My new name is Heir (Romans 8:17, Galatians 3:29)

My new name is Complete (Colossians 2:10)

My new name is Holy (Hebrews 10:10, Ephesians 1:4)

My new name is Forgiven (Psalm 103:3, Colossians 2:13)

My new name is Adopted (Ephesians 1:5)

My new name is Delight (Psalm 147:11)

My new name is Unashamed (Romans 10:11)

My new name is Known (Psalm 139:1)

My new name is Planned (Ephesians 1:11–12)

My new name is Gifted (2 Timothy 1:6, 1 Corinthians 12:11)

My new name is Enriched (2 Corinthians 8:9)

My new name is Provided For (1 Timothy 6:17)

My new name is Treasured (Deuteronomy 7:6)

My new name is Pure (1 Corinthians 6:11)

My new name is Established (Romans 16:25)

My new name is God's Work Of Art (Ephesians 2:10)

My new name is Helped (Hebrews 13:6)

My new name is Free From Condemnation (Romans 8:1)

My new name is God's Child (Romans 8:15–16)

My new name is Christ's Friend (John 15:15)

My new name is Christ's Precious Bride (Revelation 19:7, Song of Songs 7:10).

Are you frustrated by returning again and again to the same sins?

We invite you to speak out loud the following declaration (based on Romans 6 and James 4). Instead of depending on your own strength and making rules for yourself to try to keep from sinning, you can enjoy living in the reality of your new identity, Christ in you the hope of glory! (Colossians 1:27) Speak it out every day as long as it takes.

I declare that I am now a new creation in Christ. I am dead to sin and alive to God. I confess my sins [specifically name any habitual sins] and turn away from them.

I specifically declare that the sin of [specifically name any habitual sins one by one] does not rule me any longer and I renounce its control of me. Jesus, who lives in me, is my loving Master and Ruler and all that I am now belongs to Him.

Thank You, Jesus, that You have made me a saint, a holy one, so I CAN glorify You in my body. Therefore I refuse to offer my body to be used to commit unrighteousness. Instead, I submit all that I am to my Heavenly Father who raised me to life with Christ. I now gladly offer the parts of my body: my heart; eyes; ears; mouth; tongue; hands; feet; sexual organs; mind; understanding; mental powers; emotions; imagination and reasoning to God, and I choose to use these parts of my body only for righteousness, completely relying on the power of His Holy Spirit within me to accomplish this.

So I submit myself completely to God and resist the devil who must flee from me now (see James 4:7).

SESSION 4: COURAGEOUS!

WELCOME

What were some of the things you were afraid of when growing up?

WORSHIP

Jesus and all in Him is mine! John 10:10, 16:14–15

PRAYER & DECLARATION

My Father God, You are my Rock, my Shield, my Deliverer and my High Tower! How wonderful to know that I am in the palm of Your hand and no-one can snatch me away! In the strong name of Jesus my Lord. Amen.

I have not been given a spirit of fear so I turn away any spiritual attack of fear, anxiety or worry. I give them no permission to stop me hearing truth. I choose now to fix my eyes on Jesus and put my confidence in Him alone.

WORD

Focus verse: Be strong and courageous. Do not be frightened, and do not be dismayed, for the Lord your God is with you wherever you go. (Joshua 1:9)

Focus truth: We do not have to allow unhealthy fears to control us or set the agenda in our lives because God is all-powerful and everywhere-present and has given us the grace gifts of power, love and sound judgment.

Be strong and courageous

When the whole generation of the Israelites who escaped from Egypt had died wandering around the wilderness, God finally told Joshua to cross the Jordan and take the land that had been promised to them.

He said to Joshua: "Just as I was with Moses, so I will be with you. I will not leave you or forsake you. Be strong and courageous" (Joshua 1:5–6a). God then repeated Himself: "Only be strong and very courageous" and added an instruction, "being careful to do according to all the law that Moses my servant commanded you. Do not turn from it to the right hand or to the left, that you may have good success wherever you go" (Joshua 1:7–8). God then repeated Himself yet again: "Be strong and courageous. Do not be frightened, and do not be dismayed, for the Lord your God is with you wherever you go" (Joshua 1:9).

What does God say to us? The writer to the Hebrews tells us, "He has said, 'I will never leave you nor forsake you.' So we can confidently say, 'The Lord is my helper; I will not fear; what can man do to me?'" (Hebrews 13:5–6)

You are a child of God with the robe, the ring and the sandals. By His grace, you have everything you need to live a fruitful life. But fear is one of the major things that can hold you back. And if you are motivated by fear, you cannot be motivated by love.

What is fear?

Fear is an emotional reaction that triggers a physical response in our bodies that comes from the perception of impending danger or harm.

Fear is not necessarily a bad thing. We need to have a healthy fear of things that could harm us. So there are healthy fears.

Unhealthy fear

Unhealthy fear is fear that is not a reasonable response to what is happening. We may not even be aware of some of the unhealthy fears that operate in our lives. On the other hand, others can practically control us. The more severe fears are usually known as "phobias".

Unhealthy fears close our lives down. They work like the coils of a boa constrictor or python. The snake first bites its victim to gain a hold and then rapidly coils itself around its victim's torso. As the victim breathes out, the coils tighten so that its prey is unable to take as deep a breath as before. After several times of exhaling and the snake's tightening of coils, the victim suffocates, unable to breathe at all.

Most of us don't have phobias. But that does not mean we are not affected by unhealthy fears. These fears may simply have become part of our lives so that we think that's just how we are. But they keep us from being the people God created us to be. The great news is that every fear — no matter how severe — can be resolved in Christ.

PAUSE FOR THOUGHT 1

First let's pray this prayer out loud together:

Dear Heavenly Father,

I come to You as Your child and I put myself under Your protective care. Thank You that You love me so much. I confess that I have been fearful and anxious because of my lack of trust and unbelief. I have not always lived by faith in You and too often I have relied on my own strength and resources. I thank You that I am forgiven in Christ.

I choose to believe the truth that You have not given me a spirit of fear, but of power, love and sound judgment (2 Timothy 1:7). Therefore I renounce any spirit of fear. I ask You to reveal to my mind all the fears that have been controlling me. Show me how I have become fearful and the lies I have believed. I desire to live a responsible life in the power of Your Holy Spirit. Show me how these fears have kept me from doing that. I ask this so that I can confess, renounce and overcome every fear by faith in You.

In Jesus' name. Amen.

Now spend some time on your own with God and, on a separate sheet, write down the fears that you have been prone to. The following list may help you identify some of them but there will probably be others too. You will have the opportunity to work further on the fears you have identified before the end of the session.

Fear of Satan

Fear of divorce

Fear of death

Fear of not being loved by God

Fear of never being loved

Fear of not being able to love others

Fear of marriage

Fear of rejection by people

Fear of never getting married

Fear of never having children

Fear of disapproval

Fear of embarrassment

Fear of failure

Fear of financial problems

Fear of going crazy

Fear of being a hopeless case

Fear of the death of a loved one

Fear of the future

Fear of confrontation

Fear of being a victim of crime

Fear of having committed the unpardonable sin

Fear of specific people, animals, or objects

Other specific fears the Lord brings to mind

Power, love and sound judgment

> For God has not given us a spirit of fearfulness, but one of power, love and sound judgment. (2 Timothy 1:7 HCSB)

Fear robs us of power, stops us being motivated by love and steals away our sound judgment. But God has not given us that kind of cowardly spirit. He has given us a courageous one.

Power

Think about the power that raised Christ from the dead. Now that's power! That very same power lives in you! (See Romans 8:11, Ephesians 1:18–21).

But this doesn't mean you have to take a deep breath and think, "Right, I'm going to be strong." It's not your strength that matters, it's the strength of God's Holy Spirit living within you.

Love

> There is no fear in love, but perfect love casts out fear. For fear has to do with punishment, and whoever fears has not been not perfected in love. (1 John 4:18)

When you come to know and realize God's perfect love for you, the fear of His punishment is destroyed.

Sound judgment

We are all in a spiritual battle. It is essentially a battle between truth and lies, and the battleground is our mind.

Fear distorts the truth. Every unhealthy fear is based on a lie. So exercising sound judgment simply boils down to making a choice to see things the way God sees them, in other words how they really are.

For a fear to be healthy, it must be:
- present
- powerful

Neutralising just **one** of those attributes eliminates the fear.

Most of our fears relate either to a fear of death or the fear of other people.

The fear of death

Can you remove the **presence** of death? No, unless Jesus comes back first, every one of us is going to die.

What about death's other attribute... its **power**? Christ died, "that through death he might destroy the one who has the power of death, that is, the devil, and deliver all those who through fear of death were subject to lifelong slavery." (Hebrews 2:14–15)

> Death is swallowed up in victory. O death, where is your victory? O death, where is your sting? The sting of death is sin, and the power of sin is the law. But thanks be to God, who gives us the victory through our Lord Jesus Christ. (1 Corinthians 15:54–57)

The fear of people

The fear of man lays a snare, but whoever trusts in the Lord is safe.
(Proverbs 29:25)

God does not want us to remove ourselves from the **presence** of people. So, the possibility of someone not liking us and giving us the cold shoulder or worse is certainly ever **present**. Is it **powerful**? By resolving in your own mind that, if push comes to shove, you will always obey God rather than people, you remove their power. They may be present but they are no longer powerful.

PAUSE FOR THOUGHT 2

"Behind every unhealthy fear is a lie." Look at the fears below — or, better still, work on the fears that you identified in Pause For Thought 1. If someone is prone to those fears, what lies might they believe? For example, a possible lie for (1) is "Satan is more powerful than I am".

1. Fear of Satan and powers of darkness
2. Fear of the future
3. Fear of rejection
4. Fear of failure
5. Fear of confrontation
6. Fear of financial problems

What truths from God's Word can you find for each lie? For example, for (1) a good verse would be James 4:7: "Submit... to God. Resist the devil, and he will flee from you."

Living in freedom from fear

All of us will have to do battle with unhealthy fears. That's just a fact of life. Being courageous simply means that we choose to act according to the truth rather than what our fears are telling us. So let's look at a plan of action to deal with them.

1. Deal with sin issues

> I heard the sound of you in the garden, and I was afraid, because I was naked, and I hid myself. (Genesis 3:10)

Sin caused Adam to feel fear for the first time in his life. Unresolved sin issues make us vulnerable to fear.

We recommend that you make it a regular practice to go through *The Steps To Freedom In Christ*, a kind and gentle process that gives the Holy Spirit an opportunity to reveal to you every unresolved sin and then deal with it through confession and repentance.

2. Realize that God is always present AND always powerful

There is just one fear that is always healthy. The fear of God. Why? Because God is always **present** and always **powerful**.

At first, "the fear of God" sounds like we should be afraid of Him, but it is simply recognizing just who He is. And that's also the ultimate antidote to any unhealthy fear: to grasp by faith the truth that the all-knowing, everywhere-present, all-powerful, and absolutely-loving God of grace is right here with us and in us!

Even brave, courageous King David struggled with fear, but he found the way to keep that fear from overwhelming him:

> I will bless the Lord at all times; his praise shall continually be in my mouth. My soul will make its boast in the Lord; let the humble hear and be glad. O magnify the Lord with me, and let us exalt his name together!

I sought the Lord, and he answered me and delivered me from all my fears. (Psalm 34:1–4)

Cultivating a lifestyle of praise and worship will help you overcome fear.

3. Work out the lie behind the unhealthy fear

Behind every unhealthy fear is a lie. In order to root out the fear, we need to identify the lie. For example, if you find that mention of Satan and demons makes you a little scared, what lie might you believe? One possibility might be "Satan is more powerful than I am".

Ephesians 2:6 says that we are seated with Christ. Where is He? At the right hand of the Father far above all power and authority. James 4:7 tells us that if we submit to God and resist the devil, he has to flee from us.

4. Renew your mind

When a lie becomes deeply ingrained it becomes a "stronghold", a habitual way of thinking that is inconsistent with what God says in His Word.

The final step is to change your belief system so that lies are replaced with truth. Paul calls this "renewing your mind" and says that it will lead to being "transformed" (Romans 12:2). Just imagine how different life would be if you had no unhealthy fears.

"Stronghold-Busting", a structured process that will help you renew your mind, is outlined on pages 62–64.

God's Word or circumstances?

What will you choose to believe: God's Word or your circumstances?

"I will never leave you nor forsake you." (Hebrews 13:5). Never are God's words of assurance put to the test more than when our circumstances and feelings shout a message directly opposed to what God says is true. The big question: Are you going to believe what God's Word says or are you going to believe what your circumstances tell you?

Fear is the opposite of faith – and faith is simply making a choice to believe what God Himself has told us is true. In other words, it's making a choice to believe what is **already** true – and why wouldn't you want to do that? No matter what is going on around you, Jesus is in your boat!

THE GRACE COURSE | SESSION 4 | **COURAGEOUS!**

Truth & lies

Spend some time considering what lies have come to light in this session and write them down in the *Lies List* at the end of the book.

Remember that every controlling, unhealthy fear in our lives has at its root at least one lie that we have believed.

One very common lie that fuels our fear is: "If I say what I really believe, people will reject me and that will be too painful to endure. So it's safer to stay quiet."

Another is that God will not be there for us, that He will abandon us.

Some of the lies behind your fears may take a bit of unravelling. But just think how different things could be if you were to get rid of those unhealthy fears! And that's absolutely possible.

WITNESS

How would you explain to someone who doesn't yet know Jesus the difference that He makes in enabling you to live free from controlling fears?

IN THE COMING WEEK

If you have become aware that fear and anxiety are issues for you, go through two exercises, *Steps To Overcoming Fear* (on pages 65–67) and *Resolving Anxiety* (on pages 68–70). They were written by Dr Neil T. Anderson as appendices to his *Steps To Freedom In Christ* and are used by permission. If you struggle a lot with fear and anxiety, you will benefit from having a mature Christian friend to help you as you go through them. If you have completed Pause For Thought 1 in this session, you have already made a good start on the first exercise.

We have a strategy that we call "Stronghold Busting". This simple process is a straightforward way to renew your mind. This is how it works:

1. Work out the lie behind the fear (or other stronghold)

First of all, you need to work out what the lie is, as we did in Pause For Thought 2 in this session. Other people might be a great help at this point. It's helpful then to consider what effect believing the lie has had in your life — this should spur you on to tear the stronghold down. The effect of believing the lie that Satan is stronger than you, for example, might be that you let the enemy deflect you from God's purposes for you.

2. Find as many Bible verses as you can that state the truth and write them down

A good concordance or helpful church leader might come in useful here.

3. Write a prayer or declaration based on the formula:
I renounce the lie that...
I announce the truth that...

You can see some examples of completed Stronghold-Busters on the next two pages to get the idea of what this might look like.

4. Read the Bible verses and say the prayer/declaration out loud every day for 40 days

Why 40 days? Psychologists tell us that it takes around six weeks to form or break a habit. Once you have dealt with any sin issues that give the enemy a foothold in your life, a mental stronghold is simply a habitual way of thinking. Can you break a habit? Yes — but it takes some effort over a period of time. Do persevere until you have completed a total of 40 days and bear in mind that throughout most of that time, it will feel like a complete waste of time because the lie feels like truth. If you persevere, you will tear the stronghold down.

The lie: that I am not good enough or unacceptable.

Effects in my life: feeling intimidated; fearing people; compromising my convictions; changing my appearance; anxious about saying and doing the "right thing"

You did not choose me, but I chose you... (John 15:16)

[He] has put his seal on us and given us his Spirit in our hearts as a guarantee. (2 Corinthians 1:22)

He will rejoice over you with gladness; he will quiet you by his love; he will exult over you with loud singing. (Zephaniah 3:17)

Man looks on the outward appearance, but the Lord looks on the heart. (1 Samuel 16:7)

The Lord is on my side; I will not fear. What can man do to me? (Psalm 118:6)

We have been approved by God to be entrusted with the gospel, so we speak, not to please man, but to please God who tests our hearts. (1 Thessalonians 2:4)

Dear Father God, I renounce the lie that I am not good enough or unacceptable. I announce the truth that You chose me and that I have received a new heart and therefore I have Your seal of approval. Even when others are not pleased with me, You take great delight in me and Your opinion matters much more. I now choose to please You rather than other people, and rely on Your promise to be with me wherever I go as I share the good news with others. Amen.

Check off the days:

1	2	3	4	5	6	7	8	9
10	11	12	13	14	15	16	17	18
19	20	21	22	23	24	25	26	27
28	29	30	31	32	33	34	35	36
37	38	39	40					

Stronghold-Buster Example 2
Fear Of Failure

The lie: when I fail I am worth less than before.

Effects in my life: unwilling to attempt new challenges that are outside my comfort zone; being task-focused rather than people-focused; anger; competitiveness; striving for perfection

You are precious in my eyes and I love you. (Isaiah 43:4)

In [Christ] you have been made complete. (Colossians 2:10 NASB)

We are his workmanship, created in Christ Jesus for good works, which God prepared beforehand. (Ephesians 2:10)

[God] is able to do far more abundantly than all that we ask or think, according to the power at work within us. (Ephesians 3:20)

It is God who works in you, both to will and to work for his good pleasure. (Philippians 2:13)

Dear Heavenly Father, I renounce the lie that when I fail I am worth less than before. I announce the truth that I have been handcrafted by You and am precious, honoured and loved by You regardless of the success or failure of what I do. I declare that I am already fully complete in Christ and that You are working in me for Your good pleasure and to do far more abundantly than all I could ask or think. In Jesus' name. Amen.

Check off the days:

1	2	3	4	5	6	7	8	9
10	11	12	13	14	15	16	17	18
19	20	21	22	23	24	25	26	27
28	29	30	31	32	33	34	35	36
37	38	39	40					

Steps To Overcoming Fear

Analyze your fear under God's authority and guidance

Begin by praying the following prayer out loud:

Dear Heavenly Father,
I come to You as Your child and I put myself under Your protective care.
Thank You that You love me so much. I confess that I have been fearful
and anxious because of my unbelief and lack of trust. I have not always
lived by faith in You and too often I have relied on my own strength and
resources. I thank You that I am forgiven in Christ.

I choose to believe the truth that You have not given me a spirit of fear,
but of power, love and sound judgment (2 Timothy 1:7). Therefore I
renounce any spirit of fear. I ask You to reveal to my mind all the fears
that have been controlling me. Show me how I have become fearful and
the lies I have believed. I desire to live a responsible life in the power of
Your Holy Spirit. Show me how these fears have kept me from doing that.
I ask this so that I can confess, renounce and overcome every fear by faith
in You. In Jesus' name. Amen.

The following list may help you recognize some of your fears. On a separate
sheet, write down the ones that apply to you, as well as any others not on
the list that the Spirit of God has revealed to you.

- ❑ Fear of Satan
- ❑ Fear of divorce
- ❑ Fear of death
- ❑ Fear of not being loved by God
- ❑ Fear of never being loved
- ❑ Fear of not being able to love others
- ❑ Fear of marriage
- ❑ Fear of rejection by people
- ❑ Fear of never getting married
- ❑ Fear of never having children
- ❑ Fear of disapproval
- ❑ Fear of embarrassment
- ❑ Fear of failure
- ❑ Fear of financial problems
- ❑ Fear of going crazy
- ❑ Fear of being a hopeless case
- ❑ Fear of the death of a loved one
- ❑ Fear of the future
- ❑ Fear of confrontation
- ❑ Fear of being a victim of crime
- ❑ Fear of speaking to people about Jesus
- ❑ Fear of having committed the unpardonable sin
- ❑ Fear of specific people, animals, or objects
- ❑ Other specific fears the Lord brings to mind

_____

The root of any unhealthy fear is a belief that is not based in truth. These false beliefs need to be rooted out and replaced by the truth of God's Word. Take as much time in prayer as you need to discern these lies, because renouncing them and choosing the truth is a critical step towards gaining and maintaining your freedom in Christ. You have to know and choose to believe the truth in order for it to set you free. Write down the lies you have believed for every fear and the corresponding truth from the Word of God.

Ways you have been living under the control of fear

The next step is to determine how fear has prevented you from living a responsible life, compelled you to do live irresponsibly, or compromised your Christian witness. After you have gained the necessary insights into your fear, it is time to experience God's cleansing through confession and repentance (see 1 John 1:9, Proverbs 28:13). Confession is agreeing with God that what you did was sinful. Repentance is the choice to turn away from sin and to change your way of thinking. Express the following prayer for each of the controlling fears that you have analysed above:

Dear Lord,
I confess and repent of the fear of _____. I have believed (state the lie). I renounce that lie and I choose to believe the truth (state the truth). I also confess any and all ways this fear has resulted in living irresponsibly, or compromising my witness for Christ (be specific).

I now choose to live by faith in You, Lord, believing Your promise that You will protect me and meet all my needs as I live by faith in You (Psalm 27: 1; Matthew 6:33,34). In Jesus' trustworthy name. Amen.

After working through every fear the Lord has revealed to you (including their accompanying lies and sinful behaviour), then pray the following prayer:

Dear Heavenly Father,

I thank You that You are indeed trustworthy. I choose to believe You, even when my feelings and circumstances tell me to fear. You have told me not to fear, for You are with me; not to look about me anxiously, for You are my God. You will strengthen me, help me, and surely uphold me with Your righteous right hand. In Jesus' mighty name. Amen. (See Isaiah 41:10.)

Work out a plan of responsible behaviour

The next step is to face the fear and prayerfully work out a plan to overcome it. Somebody once said, "Do the thing you fear the most and the death of fear is certain." Fear is like a mirage in the desert. It seems so real until you move towards it, but then it disappears into thin air. But as long as we back away from fear, it will haunt us and grow in size, becoming like a giant.

Determine in advance what your response will be to any fear object

The fear of God is the one fear that can dispel all other fears, because God rules supreme over every other fear object, including Satan. Even though "your adversary the devil prowls around like a roaring lion, seeking someone to devour" (1 Peter 5:8), he has been defeated. "Having disarmed the powers and authorities, [Jesus] made a public spectacle of them, triumphing over them by the cross" (Colossians 2:15 NIV).

The presence of any fear object should prompt us to focus on God who is always present and all powerful. To worship God is to acknowledge and ascribe to Him His divine attributes. This keeps fresh in our minds the truth that our loving Heavenly Father is always with us and is more powerful than any enemy or circumstance.

Commit to carrying out the plan of action in the power of the Holy Spirit

Remember, you are never alone in the battle. "It is God who works in you to will and to act according to his good purpose" (Philippians 2:13 NIV).

Resolving Anxiety

Anxiety is different from fear in that it lacks an object or adequate cause. People are anxious because they are uncertain about a specific outcome or don't know what is going to happen in the future. It is normal to be concerned about things we value; not to do so would demonstrate a lack of care.

You can be temporarily anxious about an examination yet to be taken, attendance at a planned function, or the threat of an incoming storm. Such concern is normal and should ordinarily move you to responsible action. For some, the anxiety is more intense and prolonged. They struggle with a large number of worries and spend a lot of time and energy doing so. The intensity and frequency of the worrying are always out of proportion to the actual problem.

If persistent anxiety is a problem in your life, this exercise can help you to cast all your anxieties on Christ because He cares for you (see 1 Peter 5:7).

Pray

Prayer is the first step in casting all your anxiety on Christ. Remember Paul's word, "Do not be anxious about anything, but in everything by prayer and supplication with thanksgiving let your requests be made known to God" (Philippians 4:6). Ask God to guide you by expressing the following prayer:

Dear Heavenly Father,
I come to You as Your child purchased by the blood of the Lord Jesus Christ. I declare my dependence upon You, and I acknowledge my need of You. I know that apart from Christ I can do nothing. You know the thoughts and intentions of my heart and You know the situation I am in from the beginning to the end. I feel as though I am double-minded, and I need Your peace to guard my heart and my mind. I humble myself before You and choose to trust You to exalt me at the proper time in any way You choose. I place my trust in You to supply all my needs according to Your riches in glory and to guide me into all truth. I ask for Your divine

guidance so that I may fulfil my calling to live a responsible life by faith in the power of Your Holy Spirit. "Search me, O God, and know my heart! Try me and know my thoughts! And see if there be any grievous way in me, and lead me in the way everlasting!" (Psalm 139:23–24). In Jesus' precious name. Amen.

Resolve any personal and spiritual conflicts

The purpose of *The Steps To Freedom In Christ* is to help you get radically right with God and eliminate any possible influences of the devil on your mind. Remember, "The Spirit clearly says that in later times some will abandon the faith and follow deceiving spirits and things taught by demons" (1 Timothy 4:1 NIV). You will be a double-minded person if you pay attention to a deceiving spirit. You need to have the presence of God so that "the peace of God, which surpasses all understanding, will guard your hearts and your minds in Christ Jesus" (Philippians 4:7).

State the problem

A problem well-stated is half-solved. In anxious states of mind, people typically can't see the forest for the trees. Put the problem in perspective: will it matter for eternity? Generally speaking, the process of worrying takes a greater toll on a person than the negative consequences of what they worried about. Many anxious people find tremendous relief by simply having their problem clarified and put into perspective.

Separate the facts from the assumptions

People may be fearful of the facts, but not anxious. We're anxious because we don't know what is going to happen tomorrow. Since we don't know, we make assumptions. A peculiar trait of the mind is its tendency to assume the worst. If the assumption is accepted as truth, it will drive the mind to its anxiety limits. If you make presumptions about tomorrow, you will suffer the negative consequences, or stress and anxiety. "Anxiety in a man's heart weighs him down" (Proverbs 12:25). Therefore, as best as possible, verify all assumptions.

Determine what you have the right or ability to control

You are responsible only for that which you have the right and ability to control. You are not responsible for that which you don't. Your sense of worth is tied only to that for which you are responsible. If you aren't living a responsible life, you should feel anxious! Don't try to cast your **responsibility** onto Christ — He will throw it back to you. But do cast your **anxiety** onto Him, because His integrity is at stake in meeting your needs if you are living a responsible and righteous life.

List what is your responsibility

You need to commit yourself to be a responsible person and fulfil your calling and obligations in life.

The rest is God's responsibility

Your only remaining responsibility is to continue to pray and focus on the truth according to Philippians 4:6–8. Any residual anxiety is probably due to your assuming responsibilities that God never intended you to have.

SESSION 5: HUMBLE!

WELCOME

Who is the humblest person you have ever met?

WORSHIP

We love because He first loved us — 1 John 4:19.

PRAYER & DECLARATION

Dear Loving and Gracious Father, I can do nothing whatsoever of any real value without You. I offer myself to You now as a living sacrifice. Please lead me into all truth. I ask this in the humble name of Jesus Christ. Amen.

In Christ I am no longer under the Law but under grace. I choose no longer to follow "the Law" as my lord or "rules" as my ruler. I declare that Jesus Christ is my Lord and I command His enemies to leave my presence.

WORD

Focus verse: You shall love the Lord your God with all your heart and with all your soul and with all your mind. This is the great and first commandment. And a second is like it: You shall love your neighbour as yourself. On these two commandments depend all the Law and the Prophets (Matthew 22:37–40).

Focus truth: When we understand our amazing position of security in God's love, we are free to humble ourselves before Him and others so that we can work together to reach the world for Christ.

What, me? A Pharisee?

The Pharisees were originally a group of ordinary people who were radically committed to truth and to fighting against liberalism.

They ended up as shallow hypocrites. They had a grasp of truth but they didn't have a clue about grace.

Knowledge puffs up, but love builds up. (1 Corinthians 8:1)

Pride is another false motivator that keeps us from being compelled by love.

The woman caught in adultery (John 8:3–11)

The Pharisees had a good intellectual grasp of the truth. Moses did indeed command that adulterers should be put to death (see Leviticus 20:10). Jesus helped them realize that they had sinned too, just like the woman. None of them had lived up to the righteous standards of the Law.

Jesus — the only one without sin — had every right to stone her to death. Yet He didn't speak even a single word of condemnation.

Religious people are into rules. God is into relationships.

Religious people put laws above love. God makes love the supreme goal.

Religious people are most concerned about being right. God is most concerned that we be real. Only then can we be right.

Religious people make their highest aim to know the Word of God. God wants us to make our highest aim to know the God of the Word.

Why did the God of grace give the Law?

The Law was not given until hundreds of years after God's original covenant with Abraham when God made some promises:

"Fear not, Abram, I am your shield; your reward shall be very great." (Genesis 15:1)

"Look toward heaven, and number the stars, if you are able to number them." Then he said to him, "So shall your offspring be." (Genesis 15:5)

God made unconditional promises — grace promises.

And he believed the Lord, and he counted it to him as righteousness. (Genesis 15:6)

Abraham did just one thing: he chose to believe what God promised. It has always been the case that we enter into God's promises and blessing by faith, and faith alone – not by anything we do.

When the Law came, it did not supersede the grace promises God had made. It's not as if the original plan was grace and it somehow went badly wrong and had to be changed to Law.

The Law was given "because of transgressions" (Galatians 3:19. See also Romans 3:19–20.) The Law never was meant to provide a way to become acceptable to God through our own efforts. It was there to make us so aware of the awfulness of sin and its control over us, that we would understand our need of grace, our need of Christ. The Law itself was actually a means of grace!

How did Jesus fulfil the Law?

The Pharisees complained that Jesus seemed to be doing away with the Law. But He said:

"Do not think that I have come to abolish the Law or the Prophets; I have not come to abolish them but to fulfil them. For truly, I say to you, until heaven and earth pass away, not an iota, not a dot, will pass from the Law until all is accomplished..." (Matthew 5:17–18)

He became the perfect sacrifice and met all of the Law's righteous demands on our behalf

He made it possible for us not just to be **counted** as righteous, but actually to **become** righteous through and through – because of His perfect sacrifice which He paid once for all for our sin, past, present and future.

He helped us understand the true purpose of the Law

Jesus takes the Law which already seemed an impossible standard and raises the bar even higher:

"You have heard that it was said to those of old, 'You shall not murder; and whoever murders will be liable to judgment.' But I say to you that everyone who is angry with his brother will be liable to judgment." (Matthew 5:21–22a)

"You have heard that it was said, 'You shall not commit adultery.' But I say to you that everyone who looks at a woman with lustful intent has already committed adultery with her in his heart." (Matthew 5:27–28)

He showed us that we are completely incapable of meeting God's standards in our own strength.

He enabled the Law to be written on our hearts

Each time Jesus raised the bar, He moved it from a law that focussed on external behaviour to what is inside.

Although at one time, our hearts were "deceitful above all things" (Jeremiah 17:9), they are no longer.

"This is the covenant that I will make with them
   after those days, declares the Lord:
I will put my laws on their hearts,
   and write them on their minds." (Hebrews 10:16)

Now that we have become new creations in Christ, we have new hearts and
new minds. God's Law is no longer words on a tablet of stone or on a page.
It's written inside us.

PAUSE FOR THOUGHT 1

**Are there ways in which Christians today are tempted to think that they
need to obey certain "rules"?**

**Jesus says to us, "Be perfect" (Matthew 5:48). How is it possible to keep
this command?**

It's not so much about what we do, but why we do it

And he called the people to him and said to them, "Hear and understand:
it is not what goes into the mouth that defiles a person, but what comes
out of the mouth; this defiles a person.... For out of the heart come evil
thoughts, murder, adultery, sexual immorality, theft, false witness,
slander. These are what defile a person. But to eat with unwashed hands
does not defile anyone."
(Matthew 15:10–11, 19–20)

God looks not so much at what we **do** but at our hearts, our **motivation**.

Without love, no matter how good our actions or our beliefs may look,
we're just making meaningless noise — like a "noisy gong or a clanging
cymbal" (1 Corinthians 13:1).

It's not a heavy burden

"You shall love the Lord your God with all your heart and with all your soul and with all your mind. This is the great and first commandment. And a second is like it: You shall love your neighbour as yourself. On these two commandments depend all the Law and the Prophets." (Matthew 22:37–40)

The essence of the Law that God had given fitted on just two tablets of stone. The Pharisees kept expanding on what God had given so they had vast numbers of "helpful" rules and regulations. Their teaching boiled down to "shoulds" and "ought tos".

Jesus reduced the whole thing to this:

"So whatever you wish that others would do to you, do also to them, for this is the Law and the Prophets." (Matthew 7:12)

The heart of God is not to expand laws and rules. Their purpose has always been about loving God and loving others.

An intimate relationship with God is your best defence against falling into this trap.

Loving others (Philippians 2:1–11)

The crucial importance of unity

Have you experienced any of God's encouragement, comfort and love? If so, the effect of that, says Paul, should be that we love one another, that we will be in agreement with each other. Just before Jesus went to the cross, He prayed specifically for those who would come after the original disciples — that's you and me — and chose to focus on one single thing:

"I do not ask for these alone, but also for those who will believe in me through their word, that they may all be one, just as you, Father, are in me, and I in you, that they also be in us, so that the world may believe that you sent me." (John 17:20–21)

How are we going to reach this world for Christ? In the only recorded prayer that Jesus prays specifically for you, He makes it crystal clear. We need to love each other.

Humbling ourselves

Pride is about exalting yourself, puffing yourself up. The direction is **upwards**. Where are you right now? Seated in Christ at the right hand of the Father! You can't get any higher than that! When we act out of pride it shows that we don't know who we are.

Humility on the other hand is about lowering ourselves — the direction is **downwards**.

All God is asking us to do is be lower ourselves in the same way, to have the same mind, the same attitude, as Jesus had.

Humbling ourselves means that we will be prepared to be honest about our own shortcomings in relationships with others.

It means that I will humble myself before those whom God has put in leadership. I will support them, making their goals my goal too. I will work in harmony with them and not make their role any harder than it already is (see Hebrews 13:17).

As we make ourselves lower and lower, as we choose to come underneath others, we will find that we will supernaturally experience more of God's grace in our own lives.

Humble yourselves before the Lord, and he will exalt you. (James 4:10)

PAUSE FOR THOUGHT 2

On your own before God, say the following prayer:

Dear Lord,

I confess that I have believed that my ways and my preferences are better than those of other people. I ask you to reveal to me now the ways in which this sin of pride has been an issue in my life so that I might turn away from it. In Jesus' name. Amen.

Write down areas of your life where you now realize that you have been proud. Consider, for example, your attitude towards:

- Family members
- Church leaders
- Christians from other parts of the Church
- Work colleagues

Consider too if you have been proud of:

- Your understanding of Christian doctrine
- Your worldly achievements
- The things you have done for God

For each area that the Holy Spirit has brought to mind, pray this prayer:

Lord Jesus,

I confess and renounce that I was proud by/towards _____
(Say what you did and to whom). I now choose to have the same attitude You had. I humble myself before You and before other people. I declare the truth that I am in no way better than they are and I choose from now on to consider them more significant than myself. Thank You that, because I know I am Your child, I no longer have to lift myself up but can rely on You to lift me up in due course.

In Your name. Amen.

Counting others more significant than ourselves

What might it mean in practice to humble ourselves before God and others so that the world out there will know about Jesus?

Focus on the essential

First of all, just who are your Christian brothers and sisters?

If you confess with your mouth, "Jesus is Lord," and believe in your heart that God raised him from the dead, you will be saved. For it is with your heart that you believe and are justified, and it is with your mouth that you confess and are saved. (Romans 10:9–10 NIV)

Recognize that none of us has a complete understanding.

Division has become almost part of our DNA. We have an instinctive suspicion of people from other parts of the Church. Instead of coming to others with grace, we put up barriers of truth that they have to jump over.

Good theology is important but we can almost end up feeling like we're saved by good theology!

God opposes the proud, but gives grace to the humble. (James 4:6)

Come with both grace and truth

John 1:14 tells us that Jesus came "full of grace and truth". We need both. The question is which do we lead with? For the Pharisees, truth was the important thing. Jesus always held truth in balance with grace.

If we want the Church to grow and reach the people out there, don't think so much about the enemy. He's defeated. The Church is unstoppable if it is right with God:

If my people who are called by my name humble themselves, and pray and seek my face and turn from their wicked ways, then I will hear from heaven and will forgive their sin and heal their land. (2 Chronicles. 7:14).

Are we to condone things that may happen within some parts of the Church that are blatantly not in line with the Bible? No. But neither do we need to condemn them.

Only love will break down the barriers. If you make doctrine the main thing, even if you're right, you're wrong.

So how can we motivate others towards righteousness? Teach them about grace. More importantly, show them grace — humble yourself before them. Come to them the way God comes to you: not with a set of laws but with the unconditional sacrifice of His own Son.

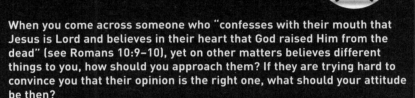

PAUSE FOR THOUGHT 3

When you come across someone who "confesses with their mouth that Jesus is Lord and believes in their heart that God raised Him from the dead" (see Romans 10:9–10), yet on other matters believes different things to you, how should you approach them? If they are trying hard to convince you that their opinion is the right one, what should your attitude be then?

What might it look like in practice for you and your church to humble yourselves before other Christians in your area? How might you play a part in that?

Uncovering lies

Have you felt the need to build yourself up by comparing yourself to others? Have you felt the need to overemphasize doctrine and "right" theology?

 WITNESS

Ask God to give you an opportunity to show love to someone this week in such a way that only He will see it.

 IN THE COMING WEEK

Say the *Declaration of Humility and Unity* (on the following page) every day to commit yourself to answering Jesus' prayer in John 17:20–23.

Declaration of Humility and Unity

Lord Jesus,

I join You in Your prayer to the Father that Your children would be one — because, like You, I want the world to believe that the Father sent You. You have said in Your Word that where there is unity, You command a blessing of life and I want to see that blessing come in full force.

Just as You — the great King of Kings — humbled Yourself by taking the form of a slave, even to the point of choosing to die a humiliating and agonising death on a cross, I choose to give up my ridiculous pretensions of being in any way righteous or right in my own strength and I humble myself before You. It's all about You and Your Kingdom, Lord, and not about me.

I choose also to humble myself before my brothers and sisters in Christ and to come to them not just with truth but with grace — just as You come to me. I choose to consider them more important than myself and to put their interests above my own. I recognize that without genuine love, anything I do is no more than a noisy gong or clanging cymbal. Even if my Christian doctrine and tradition are 100 per cent right, without love they are worth precisely nothing.

Lord, I am eager to maintain the unity of the Spirit in the bond of peace. I therefore ask You to fill me afresh with the Holy Spirit and to lead me in love. I choose to be a peacemaker not a nitpicker. I choose relationship above rules. I choose love above law. I choose to be real rather than right.

Please show me how practically I can serve and bless those You have called to different parts of Your Church.

I pray this in the name of the humble Jesus, the One who has now been lifted up to the very highest place and has the name that is above every other name.

Amen.

(Based on Psalm 133, John 1:14–17, John 17:20–23, 1 Corinthians 13, Ephesians 4:1–7, Philippians 2:1–11)

SESSION 6: FRUITFUL!

WELCOME

If you were writing a book about your life, what would you like the next chapter to be entitled?

WORSHIP

The Kingdom of God. 1 Chronicles 29:10–13, Revelation 19:6–9.

PRAYER & DECLARATION

Our Father, Your Kingdom come! Your will be done! I repent of striving in my own strength to bring about Your Kingdom purposes. Please teach me to depend upon the power of Your Life within me. I choose to make knowing You my highest goal. Amen.

I am a branch of the true vine, Jesus, a channel of His life. I choose to remain in Him so that I can bear much fruit.

WORD

Focus verse: I am the vine; you are the branches. Whoever abides in me and I in him, he it is that bears much fruit, for apart from me you can do nothing (John 15:5).

Focus truth: If we want to be fruitful, our focus needs to be not on bearing fruit but on staying close to Jesus.

How can we bear fruit?

In this session we'll be looking at how walking in God's grace is the key to living a fruitful life and we'll see that, like just about everything else to do with grace, it works in precisely the opposite way to how we naturally expect it to.

Our one responsibility is to "remain in the vine"

"I am the true vine, and my Father is the vine dresser. Every branch in me that does not bear fruit he takes away, and every branch that does bear fruit he prunes, that it may bear more fruit. Already you are clean because of the word that I have spoken to you. Abide in me, and I in you. As the branch cannot bear fruit of itself, unless it abides in the vine, neither can you, unless you abide in me. I am the vine; you are the branches. Whoever abides in me and I in him, he it is that bears much fruit, for apart from me you can do nothing." (John 15:1–5)

Two laws of the vineyard

Branches don't bear fruit because they try really hard. And neither do we.

Branches that are not attached to the vine do not and cannot bear fruit.

Christians who focus on their need to bear fruit put themselves into a law-based system of fearful, anxious performance... with the resulting guilt and shame if they fail, and pride if they appear to succeed.

But Christians who focus on simply abiding in Jesus enter into a life of "grace-rest" where, paradoxically, they bear much fruit.

We need to go through a progression in our understanding of who Jesus is. First we know Him as our **Saviour**. But we need to come to the place of surrendering to Him as **Lord**. Even that is not enough. We then need to understand that He is our very **Life** (Colossians 3:3).

Jesus modelled this: "Truly, truly, I say to you, the Son can do nothing of his own accord, but only what he sees the Father doing." (John 5:19)

Even though He was God, Jesus made it clear that He was not operating out of His "God-ness". He was modelling how God wants us to live too.

Rest in Him

Jesus made an offer, specifically to people who felt overwhelmed by the demands of trying to live up to a certain set of expectations:

"Come to me, all who labour and are heavy laden, and I will give you rest. Take my yoke upon you, and learn from me, for I am gentle and lowly in heart, and you will find rest for your souls. For my yoke is easy, and my burden is light." (Matthew 11:28–30)

Yet the picture Jesus gives us of two oxen ploughing a field looks more like hard work than rest. The rest we're talking about here does not mean lying around doing nothing. It's an internal rest that is based on faith and dependence upon God, which comes from walking close beside Him, yoked to Him and relying on His strength.

Principles of rest

Rest then work

At creation, God worked for six days and then rested on the seventh day. Adam was created on day six, so the first full day of Adam's life was the seventh day when God rested. Everything was already done. Everything he needed was on hand. There was nothing whatsoever to worry about. So he rested first and then God put him to work.

And that's the principle God wants us to work to. We rest, then we work. It's not meant to be that we work hard and then rest to recover. It's the other way around. Out of rest comes fruitful ministry.

PAUSE FOR THOUGHT 1

In what ways did Jesus' life on earth demonstrate His complete dependence upon His Father?

In what ways might our lives look different if we depended completely on God?

Don't try to control events or people

Pride and control say, "I'm the one that can make it happen. And I'll do it my way, in my time and in my strength." They keep us from true rest and from experiencing the fullness of God's provision and blessings.

Those who realize that, apart from God, they can do nothing do not need to try to control either events or people. They rest in the knowledge that their

Father God can be trusted to take care of those people and events that are outside of the realm of their control. They know that He really does work all things together for their good (Romans 8:28).

Entering into the grace-rest life

Still and quieten your soul

> O Lord, my heart is not lifted up; my eyes are not raised too high; I do not occupy myself with things too great and too marvellous for me. But I have calmed and quieted my soul, like a weaned child with its mother; like a weaned child is my soul within me. O Israel, hope in the Lord from this time forth and forevermore. (Psalm 131)

This is King David writing. Who's he kidding that he doesn't concern himself with great matters? He has to deal with life and death decisions every day! What does he mean then? It's not that he doesn't do these things. He just recognizes that if he thought he could do them in his own strength, it would be pride.

He says that the antidote to pride is that he has stilled and quietened his soul.

Like David we need to learn to still and quiet our soul, to come to the point of complete dependence on God. When we feel guilty, to lay it at the foot of the cross and walk away. When we feel ashamed, to recognize that we are new people with a new name. When the fleshly urges come, to know that they only deliver bondage and we can choose not to give in to them. When fear comes, to know that only God has the right to be feared and He is for us. When we are tempted to pride, to know that we can do absolutely nothing apart from Him.

The gateway of brokenness

God's cure for self-sufficiency is to bring us to a point of brokenness in order to teach us how absolutely dependent we are on Him, that apart from Him we really can do nothing at all of any eternal value.

He works on us as gently as He can. But it can still be painful. Jesus called it "pruning" (John 15:2). Hebrews 12 calls it "discipline".

> My son, do not regard lightly the discipline of the Lord, nor faint when you are reproved by Him; for those whom the Lord loves He disciplines, and He scourges every son whom He receives... All discipline for the moment seems not to be joyful, but sorrowful; yet to those who have been trained by it, afterwards it yields the peaceful fruit of righteousness. (Hebrews 12:5–6,11 NASB)

Scourging was what they did to Jesus with the whip prior to His crucifixion. The strongholds of self-sufficiency, self-reliance, self-satisfaction, and selfishness run very deep; they require strong measures to remove them.

We need to learn — not just in our head, but in our heart — that apart from Jesus we really can't do anything of eternal value. We need to discover Jesus as our very Life.

Even Jesus had to learn obedience through difficulties (Hebrews 5:8). There is no shortcut but, when we understand that difficult situations are actually helping us grow and bear fruit, we can learn to embrace them even if we don't enjoy them.

We don't usually experience the power of God in our lives unless we are brought to "an end of ourselves."

Whatever breaking instrument God uses in our lives, loss of reputation, misunderstanding, injustice, health issues or financial difficulties, it will be tailor-made to get down to the issues of pride and control in our lives.

Paul got to the point where he could rejoice in his difficulties because he knew they were doing him good (see 2 Corinthians 12:7–10).

PAUSE FOR THOUGHT 2

If you are willing, share with the group briefly about a time that you experienced brokenness. Did it later produce any fruit in your character or in your life?

How do you feel about the possibility that God might take you through hard times?

How do you think Paul could be "content with weaknesses, with insults, hardships, persecutions, and calamities" (2 Corinthians 12:10)? Did he really mean it?

Rising up like eagles

Eagles are huge birds. Yet they are able to climb to great heights with minimal effort. They simply jump off a high place, find some rising warm air and circle in it. They have a mechanism that means they can simply lock their wings in place.

> Even youths shall faint and be weary,
>   and young men shall fall exhausted;
>   but they who wait for the Lord shall renew their strength;
>   they shall mount up with wings like eagles;
>   they shall run and not be weary;
>   they shall walk and not faint. (Isaiah 40:30–31)

Part of resting is waiting for God, looking for the "warm air". The idea behind the Hebrew word translated here as "wait" is something like "to gather together", much as strands in a rope are bound together to make something much stronger. There's a sense that as we wait on God we are bound together with Him.

The sky's the limit!

We can do nothing without God but there's a wonderful corresponding truth: "I can do all things through him who strengthens me" (Philippians 4:13).

There are works that God has prepared just for you to do since before you were born (Ephesians 2:10). You don't know what they all are yet. No matter how huge they may be, they are all completely possible.

Yet God is much more interested in what you are **like** rather than what you **do**. He looks at the heart. The fruit of the Spirit is not external ministry, it's love, joy, peace, gentleness, self-control. All of those are character attributes. Yet as we develop those character attributes they will flow over into the things we do.

PAUSE FOR THOUGHT 3

As we come to the end of the course, share with the group what you have learned about God's grace and what impact it has made on you.

Dietrich Bonhoeffer coined the phrase "cheap grace" to describe someone who wants to enjoy all the benefits of the kingdom of God without any true heart discipleship of taking up our cross and following Christ. By now, we hope you realize that living in grace does not lead to laziness or being "soft on sin". True grace is not timid or lukewarm or soft or complacent. True grace is robust, virile, liberating and strengthening.

Jesus paid an unimaginable price so that your true **guilt** could be paid in full, to leave you completely innocent. By His grace the verdict on you has been declared: Not guilty!

Jesus became sin on your behalf and in return you became the righteousness of God. You are holy through and through. In fact you're a whole new creation with some brand new names. **Shame** is gone!

You have no need to have any unhealthy **fear** any more. By His grace, you are safe and secure in the hands of the Almighty God and He loves you.

At any time you can come and cast yourself on His mercy. Knowing that you can do nothing in your own strength but that He can do everything is a good place to be.

Here you stand, a son or daughter of the Living God, dressed in your rich robe, your ring of authority and your sandals. And you say, "God, what do You want me to do for You?" And His response might be, "There are things for you to do. But what I really want is **you**."

The very last words of God to us in His Word provide a fitting conclusion to *The Grace Course*: "The grace of the Lord Jesus be with God's people. Amen." (Revelation 22:21)

Amen!

 WITNESS

Many people are genuinely hindered from becoming a Christian because they believe they could never live up to God's standards afterwards. How would you respond to them?

 IN THE COMING WEEKS

Most of us have had the experience of coming back from a Christian conference or course feeling that it was going to be life-changing, only to realize a few weeks down the line that in fact nothing much had changed after all. If you want to be transformed by the truth you have heard on this course, there's only one way — by the renewing of your mind (Romans 12:2). So, in the coming weeks, revisit your *Lies List*. Spend time finding the corresponding truths. Write Stronghold-Busters for the key areas where you realize that your thinking is not in line with what God says is true. Persevere through each, one at a time, for 40 days.

Introduction

In the story of the two sons in Luke 15, both brothers found themselves at a distance from the father; however it was their father's desire for both of them to live in a deep, loving, close relationship with him and to experience the fullness of their inheritance as his true sons. Both were welcomed by their father to come back home again but only the younger son accepted the invitation and experienced his father's grace.

No matter where you are today, God the Father offers you this same invitation to come "home". You may want to use *The Steps To Experiencing God's Grace* simply to affirm your love for Him and enable Him to point out areas in your life that need some attention. But if you feel distant from God, if your Christian walk has become a heavy, dull, lifeless burden, or if you are losing hope that you will ever break free from slavery to sin or fear, it will help you take hold of who you are and what you have in Christ to live in God's grace where there is genuine "rest for your soul" — a different way to live!

- Love God and others because of the love you yourself receive from Him and not for any other reason.
- Experience daily victory as a consequence of the power of the Spirit within you, rather than any power or effort you have to exert.
- Find yourself becoming abundantly fruitful, bringing God much glory, by staying in a dependent relationship of rest in Him.

When we begin to see our lives from His perspective, it can be painful to realize just how far we may have wandered away from Father God. In seeking to return to that place of experiencing grace, God does not require us to try harder to please Him. Quite the opposite, for it was this "slaving away" that kept the elder son at a distance from the father.

Returning to our Father begins with having a change of mind (what the Bible calls "repentance"), and committing ourselves to believe the truth (as revealed in His Word, the Bible) about who He is, who we now are in Christ and the circumstances of our lives.

In this kind and gentle process, we would encourage you to allow the Holy Spirit to reveal not only actions, but also attitudes (including false beliefs) that have kept you from living in the daily reality of His grace and producing fruit that will last. Remember that God looks inside at the heart. Striving for acceptance with God and others through our performance can look very spiritual on the outside, but is based on beliefs that misrepresent who God is and who we are. There may not be anything obvious to point to in your actions that needs addressing (unlike the younger son), because the external behaviour itself may not look that different from those who are living in the experience of grace. But inside there is all the difference in the world. Thankfully, in Christ we have all been given a brand new heart!

We will depend completely on His ability to lead us into all truth so that we can take hold of our inheritance as God's precious children, and use the freedom He gives to offer our whole lives back to Him in love and gratitude, believing that He "is able to do far more abundantly than all that we ask or think, according to the power at work within us" (Ephesians 3:20).

So to begin, we will read the following prayer and declaration out loud:

Opening Prayer

Dear Heavenly Father,

I thank You that You love me and that Your Son died and rose again so that I could have an intimate relationship with You. I have spent too much of my life trying to gain Your acceptance when I already have it. I have related to You more on the basis of head knowledge rather than heart experience, laws rather than love.

Your Word says it was "for freedom that Christ has set us free", and I really want to take hold of that freedom! There are many ways in which I have not stood firm in Your new covenant of grace, but instead have allowed a yoke of slavery to weigh me down and wear me out. Please deliver me from all bondage in my life, and bring to my mind all the attitudes and actions that have kept me from receiving and giving away Your love. I ask that Your truth would set me free to love, worship, know, obey and serve You and others in the love and acceptance that You have extended to me in Christ. In Jesus' name I pray. Amen.

Opening declaration

In the name and authority of the Lord Jesus Christ, who has all authority in heaven and on earth, I take my stand against all His enemies who want to hinder my quest for freedom.

I refuse all fear, anxiety, doubt, confusion, deception, distraction or any other form of interference that comes from the enemies of the Lord Jesus Christ. I choose to take my place in Christ, and I declare that all His enemies have been disarmed, and that Jesus Himself came to destroy the devil's work in my life. I declare that the chains of bondage have already been broken by Christ and that I am in Him. Therefore His victory is my victory.

Step 1: Renouncing lies and choosing truth

As you have gone through The Grace Course, we have encouraged you to make a note in your *Lies List* of areas where you realize your thinking has been faulty. In this first step, God may want to reveal to you some more faulty thinking. For your freedom it is important to renounce all the lies you have become aware of during the course and instead choose to declare and believe what is really true according to God's Word.

Start by praying the following prayer:

Dear Heavenly Father,

Your Word is truth and Jesus Himself is truth. The Holy Spirit is the Spirit of truth and it is knowing the truth that will set me free. I want to know the truth, believe the truth and live in accordance with the truth. Please reveal to my mind all the lies that have kept me in bondage. I want to renounce those lies and walk in the truth of Your grace and Your acceptance of me in Christ. In Jesus' name I pray. Amen.

Affirmations of truth:

Now declare out loud these wonderful affirmations of truth! Then take some time to read them through slowly again and put a mark next to any that you know are a struggle for you to believe in your heart. You could add any that you have marked to your *Lies List* so that you can work on them later (put them in the Truth column and then try to work out the lie).

I joyfully announce the truth that I am deeply loved by God the Father:

- ☒ The Father loves me as much as He loves Jesus (John 17:23)
- ❑ The Father accepts me in Christ, just as I am (Ephesians 1:6)
- ❑ The Father has lavished His grace upon me (Ephesians 1:7–8)
- ❑ The Father purchased me with the blood of His Son (1 Corinthians 6:20)
- ❑ The Father has poured out His love on me (1 John 3:1)
- ❑ I am my Father's workmanship, His "poem" (Ephesians 2:10)
- ❑ I am the apple of my Father's eye (Zechariah 2:8)

I joyfully announce the truth that I am safe and secure in Christ:

- ❑ I am connected to Jesus like a branch to the vine (John 15:5)
- ☒ I am protected, held in Jesus' and the Father's hands (John 10:27–30)
- ❑ I am the righteousness of God in Christ, therefore in Him I do measure up! (2 Corinthians 5:21)
- ❑ I am accepted in Christ to the glory of God (Romans 15:7)
- ❑ I died with Christ to the rule of sin and have been raised up to live a new life (Romans 6:3–4)
- ❑ I died to the law through the body of Christ (Romans 7:4)
- ☒ I will never be deserted or forsaken by Christ (Hebrews 13:5)

I joyfully announce the truth that the Holy Spirit lives in me and He is my strength:

- ❑ I am the Temple of the Holy Spirit who was given to me by my Father (1 Corinthians 6:19)
- ❑ I am sealed by the Spirit who was given to me as a pledge of my full inheritance in Christ (Ephesians 1:13)

- ❑ I am led by the Spirit of adoption and am no longer a slave to fear; He enables me to cry out "Abba! Father!" (Romans 8:14–15)
- ❑ I have been baptized by the Holy Spirit and placed into the body of Christ as a full member (1 Corinthians 12:13)
- ❑ I have been given spiritual gifts by the Holy Spirit (1 Corinthians 12:7,11)
- ✎ I can walk by the Holy Spirit instead of giving in to the lusts of my flesh (Galatians 5:16–18,25)

The main lies you will work on are those that you have already uncovered. It may also help you to look through the table below where we have listed common lies together with possible reasons why people believe those lies (though there may be others), as well as some of the likely results in a person's life. Sometimes it helps to uncover a lie by working backwards and looking at the "Result" column first to see if you recognize any of the symptoms of believing a particular lie. If you do recognize a lie as applying to you, put a mark beside it and add it your *Lies List*.

LIE	POSSIBLE REASON	RESULT	
I can't do anything right and my best is not good enough.	Continual criticism and put-downs. Coming from an overly strict family background.	Instability, indecision, critical or judgmental spirit, unhealthy competition.	✗
I must measure up to certain standards in order to be a valuable and worthwhile person.	Living under a system of performance-based acceptance.	Perfectionism, drivenness, anxiety, insecurity, control, manipulation of people and circumstances.	✗
I'm unlovable, worthless, unattractive and unwanted.	Receiving little or no affection or healthy physical touch.	Withdrawing from people, or using my body to get attention and affection.	

LIE	POSSIBLE REASON	RESULT	
I am guilty, evil, dirty, defiled, not good enough for a relationship with God and/or other people.	Physical, verbal, emotional, sexual abuse.	Feelings of guilt and shame, hiding and covering up or living according to the lie (sexual promiscuity, addictions etc.).	
I am unimportant, unwanted, abandoned, outcast, rejected.	Being ignored or rejected. Emotional neglect.	Trying hard to please, dropping out, behaving badly to gain attention, anger, rage, bitterness, depression.	
I am incompetent, weak, inadequate or untrustworthy. "I can't do it."	Past failures. Overprotection or smothering.	Perfectionism, fear, feelings of inadequacy.	
I am _____ (the negative names they call me or I call myself).	Cursing, name-calling or labelling.	Self-hatred, inferiority, attacking others.	
I am (we are) better than others.	Repeatedly hearing others (who are not "like us") being put down and criticized.	Boasting, arrogance, putting others down, separatism, self-righteousness.	

Lies List

Now turn to your *Lies List* in the back of this book. Spend some time filling in the "Truth" column if you haven't already done so.

Below is a suggested prayer to renounce the lies that you have believed about yourself and the false identities that hinder your relationship with God and others. At the appropriate place in the prayer, include all the lies you have marked on your *Lies List*.

Take as much time as you need and pray it from the heart. As you come to grips with how these lies have controlled your life, it may be very emotional for you. Don't feel you have to maintain emotional control during this time.

Allow the emotions and feelings to surface, expressing and releasing them to the Lord in prayer. The Lord is a refuge for you!

Dear Heavenly Father,

I thank You for showing me the lies I have believed about myself and my life. I can see how damaging they have been to me and the negative effects they have had on my behaviour.

I renounce the lie that _____ (state the lie or lies that you have believed). I announce the truth that _____ (state the truth from the Bible).

I confess I have believed all these things that are contrary to Your truth and I specifically renounce all the ways the lies have caused me to live in guilt, shame, fear and pride.

I thank You for Your total forgiveness and cleansing according to 1 John 1:9 which says that if we confess our sins, You are faithful and just to forgive us our sins and to cleanse us from all unrighteousness. I now choose to draw near to You my Father, not as a slave trying to earn Your acceptance, but trusting that I am already loved and accepted as Your precious child.

In Jesus' name. Amen.

Step 2: False expectations

The elder brother mistakenly believed that he had to earn anything that would come from his father but the truth was that he could have been enjoying everything the father had all along. We're going to ask God to reveal to us all of the false expectations and standards that we have felt we have had to meet in order to feel good about ourselves, to measure up or to be acceptable. Pray the following prayer:

Loving Father,

I thank You that in Christ all of Your expectations of me have been fully met, (Romans 8:4) and that You have forgiven me all my transgressions and cancelled out my certificate of debt by nailing it to the cross (Colossians 2:13–14). I confess that I have believed the lie that I have needed something more than Christ in order to gain or maintain acceptance with You and others. Please would You reveal to me now all the expectations, standards and demands that I have been living under, by which I have sought to become more acceptable and feel less guilty, so that I can return in simple faith to relying just on Christ's work on my behalf.

I ask this in the name of Jesus Christ, who died for me. Amen.

Now spend time just between you and God considering the following areas and write down the specific expectations you have felt:

❑   Expectations you wrongly believed were from God

❑   Expectations from parents and family

❑   Expectations from teachers

❑   Expectations from churches and church leaders

☐ Expectations from employers

☒ Other false expectations: _Expectations from myself_

Then for each false expectation that you have listed, say the following:

I renounce the lie that I have to live up to the expectation of
Myself **in order to feel good enough, valued or accepted. Thank You, Lord Jesus, that in You I meet all of God's expectations and that nothing I could do could make You love me more or love me less. Amen.**

You may like to write the false expectations you have believed on a separate sheet of paper and then tear it up to symbolize that you choose from now on to trust in Jesus alone to make you right with God. Then move on in freedom and confidence!

The truth about our Father God

Having a wrong view of God's character and His expectations of us will hinder the development of a close intimate relationship with Him. The next part of this step is designed to give you an opportunity to renounce out loud the lies you have believed about God, and to affirm the truth about His character. The Bible references are there for you to look up at home. We encourage you to do this, especially those truths that are hard for you to receive today. Meditation upon the truths of who God is can be one of the most important aspects of your freedom and healing in Christ.

I renounce the lie that my Father God is:	I joyfully accept the truth that my Father God is:
✘ distant and uninterested in me.	intimate and involved (see Psalm 139:1–18).
insensitive and uncaring.	kind and compassionate (see Psalm 103:8–14).
stern and demanding.	accepting and filled with joy and love (see Romans 15:7; Zephaniah 3:17).
passive and cold.	warm and affectionate (see Isaiah 40:11; Hosea 11:3–4).
✘ absent or too busy for me.	always with me and eager to be with me (see Hebrews 13:5; Jeremiah 31:20; Ezekiel 34:11–16).
impatient, angry or never satisfied with what I do.	patient and slow to anger and delights in those who put their hope in His unfailing love (see Exodus 34:6; 2 Peter 3:9, Psalm 147:11).
mean, cruel or abusive.	loving and gentle and protective (see Jeremiah 31:3; Isaiah 42:3; Psalm 18:2).
trying to take all the fun out of life.	trustworthy and wants to give me a full life; His will is good, perfect and acceptable for me (see Lamentations 3:22–23; John 10:10; Romans 12:1–2).

I renounce the lie that my Father God is:	I joyfully accept the truth that my Father God is:
controlling or manipulative.	full of grace and mercy, and gives me freedom to fail (see Hebrews 4:15–16; Luke 15:11–16).
condemning or unforgiving.	tender-hearted and forgiving; His heart and arms are always open to me (see Psalm 130:1–4; Luke 15:17–24).
nit-picking or a demanding perfectionist.	committed to my growth and proud of me as His growing child (see Romans 8:28–29; Hebrews 12:5–11; 2 Corinthians 7:14).

I am the Apple of His Eye!

Now look back over the list and mark any truths that you find difficult to believe. We would encourage you to look up the Bible references and then use the following prayer to process these truths at a deeper level. You may like to continue to use the prayer every day until you know the truths in your heart.

Dear Heavenly Father,

I confess and repent of believing the lie(s) that You are _____ (list the specific lies you have believed). I thank You for Your gracious and merciful forgiveness. I choose to believe the truth(s) that You are _____ (list the corresponding truths). In light of those truths, please change the way I worship, pray, live and serve, empowering me now by the fullness of the Holy Spirit.

In Jesus' name. Amen.

Step 3: Confessing sin

When we believe lies about ourselves, God and others, it is inevitable that we commit sin. Sin is "missing the mark" or falling short of God's glory in our lives (Romans 3:23). Though the wages of sin is death, "the free gift of God is eternal life in Christ Jesus our Lord" (Romans 6:23). For believers there is now **no** condemnation (Romans 8:1). As we confess our sins (agree with God about them), we experience His forgiveness and cleansing (1 John 1:9).

Below are categorized some areas of particular weakness for people who struggle to live in God's grace. Following the opening prayer and lists of sins, there is a suggested prayer of confession for you to pray out loud from the heart. To begin this step, ask the Lord to reveal to your mind all the sins you need to confess by praying this prayer:

Dear Heavenly Father,

You have told me in Your Word to "put on the Lord Jesus Christ, and make no provision for the flesh in regard to its lusts" (Romans 13:14 NASB). I confess I have often given in to fleshly lusts that wage war against my soul. I thank You that in Christ, my sins are already forgiven but I acknowledge that I have broken Your holy law and given the devil a chance to wage war in my body.

I come to You now to confess and renounce these sins of the flesh so that I might be cleansed and set free from the bondage of sin. Please reveal to my mind all the sins of the flesh I have committed and the ways I have grieved the Holy Spirit.

In Jesus' name. Amen.

Areas to consider:

Performance:

- ☐ Trying to keep God's commands in order to gain His acceptance or favour
- ☒ Trying to keep God's commands in my own strength
- ☒ Trying to measure up to the standards of others in order to be accepted
- ☐ Being driven to work harder and harder in order to achieve
- ☒ Believing that achievement is the means of gaining personal happiness and a sense of worth
- ☐ Centring my life around keeping laws and rules rather than knowing God

Perfectionism:

- ☒ Living in the fear of failure
- ☐ Being afraid of going to hell because I have not kept God's laws perfectly
- ☐ Being unable to accept God's grace because I think I need to be "punished" (even though Jesus paid for all my sins in full on the cross)
- ☐ Being obsessed with doing everything perfectly and keeping things in exact order
- ☐ Being overly concerned with minor details or minor flaws in others
- ☐ Having unreasonable expectations of perfection in others
- ☐ Being angry at others when they disrupt my neatly controlled world
- ☐ Punishing others when they are not perfect
- ☐ Being unable to experience joy and satisfaction in life unless something I do is perfect

Pride and prejudice:

- ❏ Thinking I am more spiritual, devoted, humble, or devout than others
- ❏ Thinking that my church, denomination or group is better than others
- ❏ Not being willing to associate with others who are different (having an independent spirit)
- ❏ Elevating religious opinions to the level of inflexible convictions
- ❏ Not being willing to soften religious opinions in order to promote love, peace, and unity among true brothers and sisters in Christ
- ❏ Finding it hard to admit that I am wrong (thinking I am always right) or feeling the need to prove to others that I am right

Judgmentalism:

- ❏ Having a critical spirit towards worship styles, music, sermons, other people's clothes etc; being quick to criticize and critique
- ❏ Judging others (criticising their motives and character)
- ❏ Criticising ministers and Christian leaders
- ❏ Intolerance of anyone with different views and convictions
- ❏ Labelling of others, placing them in religious categories, writing them off

Being overly rigid:

- ❏ Being rigid in beliefs about which sincere Christians disagree
- ❏ Clinging to traditions in church that are not Bible-based and that are not essential to reaching the current generation with the gospel
- ❏ Stubbornness and resistance to new things in church
- ❏ Being unwilling to listen to new ideas

Power and domination:

- ❑ Using guilt and shame tactics to get others to do what I want or think best
- ❑ Expecting or demanding that others attend every church service, function etc.
- ❑ Controlling others by means of strong personality, overbearing persuasion, fear or intimidation
- ☒ Experiencing anxiety when I am not able to be in control
- ❑ Finding security in rules, regulations and standards rather than in the Lord
- ❑ Being more concerned about controlling others than developing self-control
- ❑ Being driven to attain positions of power in order to gain control and accomplish my agenda (however worthy that agenda may be)
- ❑ Feeling unhealthy responsibility for the lives and well-being of others

Pleasureless living:

- ❑ Living a joyless life of duty and obligation
- ❑ Feeling guilty for experiencing pleasure or being secretive in pursuing it
- ❑ Being unable to relax and rest
- ❑ Suffering from workaholism
- ☒ Being strongly attracted to (or giving in to) illegal substances, illicit sex, pornography etc, in order to escape or to find some gratification

As the Holy Spirit reveals these (and other) sins of the flesh to you, confess and renounce them by praying the following prayer out loud from the heart:

Dear Heavenly Father

I confess that I have sinned by _____ (name the sins). I agree that these attitudes and actions are not proper for a child of Yours, therefore I renounce them all. I thank You for Your forgiveness and I now commit myself to being filled by the Holy Spirit every day so that I might become more like Christ. I choose to allow You to develop the fruit of the Spirit in my life, which is "love, joy, peace, patience, kindness, goodness, gentleness, faithfulness and self-control".

In Jesus' holy name I pray. Amen.

(See Galatians 5:22–23)

Pride

As you have considered these sins of the flesh, you may have become aware that you have sometimes been proud. Remember that God opposes the proud and that humility is the key to unity and to answering Jesus' prayer in John 17 that we would be one. Take this opportunity to consider where pride has been an issue in your life by praying the following prayer:

Dear Lord,

I confess that I have believed that my ways and my preferences are better than those of other people. I ask You to reveal to me now the ways in which this sin of pride has been an issue in my life so that I might turn away from it.

In Jesus' name. Amen.

Write down areas of your life where you now realize that you have been proud. Consider, for example, your attitude towards:

- ☒ Family members
- ❑ Church leaders
- ❑ Christians from other parts of the Church
- ❑ Work colleagues

Consider too if you have been proud of:

- ❑ Your understanding of Christian doctrine
- ❑ Your worldly achievements
- ❑ The things you have done for God

For each area that the Holy Spirit has brought to mind, pray this prayer:

Lord Jesus,

I confess and renounce that I was proud by/towards
_____ (say what you did and to whom). I now choose to
have the same attitude You had. I humble myself before You and before
other people. I declare the truth that I am in no way better than they are
and I choose from now on to consider them more significant than myself.
Thank you that, because I know I am Your child, I no longer have to lift
myself up but can rely on You to lift me up in due course. In Your name.
Amen.

Receiving Your New Name

Being caught in sin can make us see ourselves very differently from who we
are in Christ. Many of us have been deeply affected by names and labels
that we have picked up, which continue to shape our understanding of who
we are, even after we have become children of God. Allow the Holy Spirit to
reveal your new identity in Christ by writing your new name deep in your
heart, so that by faith you will receive the truth and become in behaviour
the person God has already made you in your inner person.

Once you have read the opening prayer, take some time to read and declare
God's truth out loud, expecting Him to reveal to you a specific new name He
wants you to receive as you do!

Loving Father,

I confess that I have not always allowed the truth of Your Word to be the
foundation for how I see myself. However, today I choose to believe what
You say is now true of me in Christ regardless of my feelings and past

experiences. I thank You that You have made me new through the work of Jesus on the cross, and that I have been made worthy to enter in and enjoy a deep relationship with You and others.

You promise in Your Word that You will give Your children a new name that Your mouth will speak (Isaiah 62:2). As I declare the truth of my new identity, I ask You to speak into my heart by Your Spirit a specific new name that You want me to receive today. I choose to receive it by faith. From today, Father, I ask that You will continue to establish me in my new identity, not just in my heart but in my actions too, bringing You much glory and praise.

In the name of Jesus. Amen.

Mighty Warrior

I declare the truth that:

My new name is Beloved (Colossians 3:12)
My new name is Beautiful (Psalm 149:4, Song of Songs 4:1)
My new name is Chosen (Ephesians 1:4)
My new name is Precious (Isaiah 43:4)
My new name is Safe (1 John 5:18)
My new name is Loved (1 John 4:10)
My new name is Clean (John 15:3)
My new name is Presentable (Hebrews 10:22)
My new name is Protected (Psalm 91:14, John 17:15)
My new name is Welcomed (Ephesians 3:12)
My new name is Heir (Romans 8:17, Galatians 3:29)
My new name is Complete (Colossians 2:10)
My new name is Holy (Hebrews 10:10, Ephesians 1:4)
My new name is Forgiven (Psalm 103:3, Colossians 2:13)
My new name is Adopted (Ephesians 1:5)
My new name is Delight (Psalm 147:11)
My new name is Unashamed (Romans 10:11)
My new name is Known (Psalm 139:1)
My new name is Planned (Ephesians 1:11–12)
My new name is Gifted (2 Timothy 1:6, 1 Corinthians 12:11)
My new name is Enriched (2 Corinthians 8:9)

✦ My new name is Provided For (1 Timothy 6:17)
My new name is Treasured (Deuteronomy 7:6)
My new name is Pure (1 Corinthians 6:11)
My new name is Established (Romans 16:25)
My new name is God's Work Of Art (Ephesians 2:10)
My new name is Helped (Hebrews 13:6)
My new name is Free From Condemnation (Romans 8:1)
My new name is God's Child (Romans 8:15–16)
My new name is Christ's Friend (John 15:15)
My new name is Christ's Precious Bride (Revelation 19:7, Song of Songs 7:10).

For the name(s) that God has particularly impressed upon you, say:

Thank You, Father God, that I am _A MIGHTY WARRIOR_ (declare your new name — there may be more than one!)

We strongly encourage you to continue declaring in faith this precious truth every morning for at least the next 40 days and at other times throughout the day whenever you feel attacked in your mind by the lies of the enemy.

Step 4: Forgiveness

It is a very human thing to experience anger towards those who have hurt or offended us. This is especially true when those people we expected and needed to model and teach us love, grace and acceptance — and to care for and protect us — did not do so. The pain we feel in our lives because of the physical, verbal, emotional, sexual and spiritual abuse we have suffered can be devastating.

Although we cannot reverse the wrongs done to us, we can be free from their hold over our lives. Jesus Christ can enter into those wounded places and begin to heal the damage done to our souls. That healing begins when we make a choice to forgive from our hearts.

Paul writes, "Let all bitterness and wrath and anger and clamour and slander be put away from you, along with all malice. Be kind to one another, tender-hearted, forgiving each other, just as God in Christ also has forgiven you." (Ephesians 4:31–32)

Christ forgave us when He took the eternal consequences for our sins upon Himself. When we forgive others we are agreeing to live with the temporary consequences of their sin. It seems unfair, but the only real choice we have is between living with the consequences in the bondage of bitterness, or in the freedom of forgiveness.

To forgive means to choose not to hold someone's sin against them any more. It means cancelling the debt and letting them off your hook, though knowing they are not off God's hook. It is choosing to release the person and what they did into God's hands, trusting Him to deal with that person justly – something you are simply not able to do. It is believing that Jesus died for the sin of the person who sinned against you. And it is letting go of the right to seek revenge.

Forgiveness means that you accept that what was done to you by the offender cannot be changed. It involves recognising that holding onto your anger hurts you the most, so forgiveness is necessary for your freedom.

Forgiving from the heart

Do you want to stop the pain? Do you want Jesus' healing in your life? Do you want to have a deeper experience of God's love in your own heart? Then you need to forgive from the heart. To forgive from the heart means you mean what you say and you mean what you pray. How do you come to the point of sincerity? By acknowledging the hurt and the hate you feel. Then remembering that you are not deserving of God's forgiveness either, but that He freely gave it to you through Christ. It is experiencing God's forgiveness in your own life that frees you to forgive others.

Forgiving someone from the heart means that you are honest with God and yourself about how the offence(s) made you feel. You allow Jesus to bring to the surface the feelings that you have held inside for so long, so that He can begin to heal those emotional hurts and pain.

Begin this crucial step by praying the following prayer:

Dear Heavenly Father,

I thank You for the riches of Your kindness, forbearance and patience towards me, knowing that Your kindness has led me to repentance. I confess that I have not shown that same kindness and patience towards those who have hurt and offended me. Instead I have held on to my anger, bitterness and resentment towards them. I realize too, that at times I have been hard on myself, being unwilling to forgive myself and living with a heavy burden of regret.

Please bring to my mind all the people I need to forgive in order that I may do so now.

In Jesus' name I pray. Amen.

(See Romans 2:4)

Making the choice

We encourage you to make a complete list (by name if possible) of all the people or groups of people the Lord brings to your mind, whom you need to forgive. Use a separate sheet of paper. Here are some suggestions:

- Parents and other family members who abused me in any way or caused me to believe I was worthless and unlovable or valuable only when I "performed well".
- Ministers and other church leaders who hurt me by fostering a performance-based rather than a grace-based environment.
- School teachers or officials who were harsh, critical or judging.
- Other people who stifled the free expression of grace or spiritual liberty in my life and who forced me to conform to unattainable standards.
- Others who were used by the enemy to rob me of freedom and joy, including any perpetrators of abuse or neglect.
- Myself; for imposing heavy burdens or unattainable standards upon my family; for leading or influencing my church into legalism; for attacking those teaching freedom and grace; for being hurtful, hateful, critical or judgmental towards others; for robbing others of freedom and joy by my attitudes, words and actions.
- God Himself. Although He has done no wrong, we may have had false expectations of what He was going to do in our lives or questions about why He allowed certain things to happen. It is vital for our freedom that we acknowledge these feelings (after all, He already knows about them and they don't make a jot of difference to His love for us!), make a choice to put our trust in Him again even though we may feel He abandoned us in our time of need, because the truth is He has never left us or forsaken us (Hebrews 13:5) and He "does all things well" (Mark 7:37).

Use the prayer below as a beginning point to choose to forgive those on your list. When you are ready, start with the first person on your list, forgiving him or her from your heart for every painful memory the Lord brings to your mind. Once you can't think of anything else to forgive that person for, move onto then next one on your list, and so on. Don't worry if it takes a long time.

Dear Heavenly Father,

I choose to forgive _____ (specifically say the name of the person or group) for _____ (be specific in what they did or failed to do) which made me feel _____ (be honest in expressing how you felt or still feel.)

Once you have forgiven all those on your list, pray a blessing over them:

Dear Heavenly Father,

I choose no longer to seek revenge or to hold onto my bitterness towards _____ (names). I thank You for setting me free from the bondage of my bitterness. I now ask You to bless _____ (names).

In Jesus' name. Amen.

Step 5: Freedom from fear

In this step we will be asking God to reveal any unhealthy fears. These are fears that we wrongly believe are both present and potent. Begin by praying the following prayer out loud:

Dear Heavenly Father,

I come to You as Your child. I put myself under Your protective care and acknowledge that You are the only legitimate fear object in my life. I confess that I have been fearful and anxious because of my lack of trust and unbelief. I have not always lived by faith in You and too often I have relied on my own strength and resources. I thank You that I am forgiven in Christ.

I choose to believe the truth that You have not given me a spirit of fear, but of power, love and a sound mind (2 Timothy 1:7). Therefore I renounce any spirit of fear. I ask You to reveal to my mind all the unhealthy fears that have been controlling me. Show me how I have become fearful and the lies I have believed. Open the eyes of my heart to Your wonderful truths. I desire to live a responsible life in the power of Your Holy Spirit. Show me how these fears have kept me from doing that. I ask this so that I can confess, renounce and overcome every fear by faith in You.

In Jesus' name. Amen.

The following list may help you recognize some of the unhealthy fears that have been hindering your walk of faith. Mark the ones that apply to you, as well as any others not on the list that the Spirit of God has revealed to you.

- ❏ Fear of Satan
- ❏ Fear of divorce
- ☒ Fear of death
- ❏ Fear of not being loved by God
- ❏ Fear of never being loved
- ❏ Fear of not being able to love others
- ❏ Fear of marriage
- ❏ Fear of rejection
- ❏ Fear of never getting married
- ❏ Fear of never having children
- ❏ Fear of disapproval
- ❏ Fear of embarrassment
- ☒ Fear of failure

- ☒ Fear of financial problems
- ❏ Fear of going crazy
- ❏ Fear of being a hopeless case
- ☒ Fear of the death of a loved one
- ❏ Fear of the future
- ❏ Fear of confrontation
- ☒ Fear of being a victim of crime
- ❏ Fear of having committed the unpardonable sin
- ❏ Fear of specific animals or objects
- ❏ Fear of people
- ❏ Other specific fears the Lord brings to mind

Remember, behind every unhealthy fear is a lie, a belief that is not based on what is actually true. These false beliefs need to be rooted out and replaced by the truth of God's Word. It will help you hugely if you are able to discern these lies, because renouncing them and choosing the truth is a critical step towards gaining and maintaining your freedom in Christ. You have to know and choose to believe the truth in order for it to set you free.

When you are ready, write down the lies you have believed for every fear that you have marked on the table on the next page or, if there are too many, use a separate piece of paper. Then write out the corresponding truths from the Word of God.

This is not easy because the lies seem true and have probably been with you a long time. If you can, get some help from a mature Christian friend.

Write any lies that you identify on the *Lies List* at the back of this book.

FEAR	LIE	TRUTH
[Example:] Failure	If I fail it will make me worthless.	"I am precious in his sight and he loves me" (Isaiah 43:4).
Fear of financial Problems	my future is reliant on my financial position	my future is set in Christ Jesus
Fear of death of a loved one	God will take people away from me as punishment	
Fear of death	Dani will not be able to cope if I die.	Dani is Gods child + he loves her.

It's now time to experience God's cleansing through confession and repentance (see 1 John 1:9; Proverbs 28:13). Confession is agreeing with God that what you did was sinful. Repentance is the choice to turn away from sin and change your way of thinking. Express the following prayer for each of the controlling fears that you have analysed above:

Dear Lord,

I confess and repent of the fear of _____ . I have believed _____ (state the lie). I renounce that lie and I choose to believe the truth _____ (state the truth). I also confess any and all ways this fear has resulted in living irresponsibly, or compromising my witness for Christ.

I now choose to live by faith in You, Lord, believing Your promise that You will protect me and meet all my needs as I live by faith in You (Psalm 23:1, 27:1; Matthew 6:33–34).

In Jesus' trustworthy name. Amen.

Fear of people

We are now going to allow the Holy Spirit to search us further in one specific area of fear; that of the fear of people. Proverbs 29:25 says, "The fear of man lays a snare, but whoever trusts in the Lord is safe." Fearing man ultimately leads to pleasing people — and that indeed is bondage. People-pleasers find themselves more and more concerned about what others around them think, because they wrongly believe that their personal worth and happiness are dependent upon the acceptance or approval of others.

When we make it our goal to keep people happy, we end up becoming enslaved to them and we remove ourselves from the safety and security of serving Christ alone (Galatians 1:10). To allow the Holy Spirit to examine your heart in this area, begin by praying:

Dear Heavenly Father

I know that I have not always walked by faith, but have allowed the fear of people to control me. I have been too concerned about gaining approval from others, and I have been led astray from a simple pure devotion to Christ. I want to walk in a healthy fear and awe of You Lord, and not of people. Thank You for Your forgiveness. I now ask You to bring to my mind the specific ways that I have allowed the fear of other people to control me.

In Jesus' name I pray. Amen.

Now mark on the following list areas that the Holy Spirit is revealing to you:

- ❑ I have been afraid to say what I really think or feel for fear of being reprimanded, ridiculed, or rejected
- ❑ I have changed my manner of dressing, make-up, hair styles to prevent being reprimanded
- ❑ I am afraid to say "No" when asked to do something for fear of experiencing disapproval or anger
- ❑ I am often tired and on the verge of burn-out because of my inability to say "No"

- ❑ I resent feeling "used" but I can't seem to bring myself to set healthy boundaries in my life
- ❑ I find myself easily intimidated by strong personalities
- ❑ I constantly need the affirmation of other people in order to feel happy, significant or worthwhile
- ❑ If I don't get affirmation, I can easily become depressed, discouraged and give up
- ❑ I don't handle criticism well; it is painful because it makes me feel like a failure
- ❑ I will do almost anything to gain the approval of important people in my life
- ❑ I make sure that others know about the "good" things I have done
- ❑ I have found myself lying in order to cover things up in my life that might result in disapproval from others
- ❑ I have been more concerned with following man-made traditions in our church than with obeying God's Word
- ❑ Other ways I have allowed the fear of others to control me:

Now work through every fear you have marked using the prayer below:

Dear Heavenly Father

I realize now that my life has been influenced by the fear of people, seeking to please them rather than discerning and doing Your will. I realize that is sin. I specifically confess now the sins that _____ (list the sins the Lord revealed to you in the list above).

Thank You for Your gracious forgiveness. I ask You to strengthen me so that I will fear no-one but You. Empower me by Your Spirit to learn what pleases You and to do it, regardless of what others might think.

I thank You that You already love, accept and approve of me, so that I don't have to go looking for those things in other people. It is nice when I get them, but let them be by-products of having pleased You first.

In Jesus' name I pray. Amen.

After working through every fear the Lord has revealed to you, pray the following prayer:

Dear Heavenly Father,

I thank You that You are indeed trustworthy. I choose to believe You, even when my feelings and circumstances tell me to fear. You have told me not to fear, for You are with me; not to look about me anxiously, for You are my God. You will strengthen me, help me, and surely uphold me with Your righteous right hand.

In Jesus' mighty name. Amen.

(See Isaiah 41:10)

Step 6: Surrendering to God

At the end of Session 1, we asked if you were ready to make a commitment to God to be His bondslave, to serve Him not because you are in any way compelled to, but simply because you love Him. The following exercise and prayer are designed to make this commitment real and personal for you. It is a scary thing to think about surrendering all our "rights" and putting ourselves unreservedly into the hands of another — even if it is God! Remember that He has already shown the depth of His commitment to us by dying for us. To surrender ourselves fully into the hands of our loving Father puts us in the place of complete security.

In our society we are so focused on our "rights". A bondslave, however, surrenders all rights in order to serve his master. We are bondslaves of Christ — but we are also children of God, who have the promise that "all things belong to us and we belong to Christ; and Christ belongs to God" (1 Corinthians 3:22–23 NASB). When we lose (surrender) who we are in the natural, we find who we really are in Christ.

In truth we really have only one right: "But to all who did receive him, who believed in his name, he gave the right to become children of God" (John 1:12). To begin this step, say the following prayer:

Dear Heavenly Father,

I acknowledge that You have been a faithful God to me and will continue to be true to who You are, no matter what my circumstances or how I feel (Lamentations 3:22–23).

I confess that I have not always trusted that You have my best interests at heart, or that You can be relied upon to come through on Your promises. I repent of any doubts I may have had concerning Your character and all the ways I have tried to take my life into my own hands.

Please show me all the areas where I have held my life back from You or where I have not given You the right to act in my life as You desire. I now ask You to help me take a step of greater trust and dependence on You by surrendering all I am and all I have to You. In Jesus' name. Amen

What rights do you specifically need to surrender to God now?

- ☐ Living my life in my own strength
- ☒ Relying on my own resources
- ☐ Saying what I want to say when I want to say it
- ☐ Going where I want to go whenever I please
- ☐ Living wherever I want to live
- ☐ Having the kind of job I want
- ☒ Having the kind of financial security I desire
- ☐ Being single or married
- ☐ Having the number (and sex) of children I want to have
- ☐ Having all of my children grow up to love and walk with the Lord
- ☐ Being right all the time
- ☐ Being always loved, accepted, and understood by people
- ☐ Having the friends I want
- ☐ Being used by God in specific ways
- ☐ Being in control or in charge
- ☒ Having a good reputation
- ☒ Knowing the will of God all the time
- ☐ Being able to "fix" people or circumstances around me
- ☐ Having good health
- ☐ Being free from pain or suffering
- ☐ Having the respect and support of people around me
- ☐ Being always shielded from the abuse and neglect of others
- ☐ Receiving forgiveness from those that I have hurt
- ☐ Being spared heartache, crisis and tragedy
- ☐ Engaging in sinful practices out of anger towards, or in rebellion against, those who have hurt me
- ☐ Other things the Lord is laying on my heart:

Now pray the following prayer, telling God all the "rights" that you are choosing to surrender to Him:

Dear Heavenly Father

In the past I have claimed these rights as mine _____
**(lay down each specific right here). But now I lay them down before You
and present myself to You as a living sacrifice, Your bondslave. I am no
longer my own. I choose to surrender all my selfish rights to You, the One
who has loved me and given up Your Son for me.**

**While I accept my responsibility to follow Your good, pleasing and perfect
will for me by the power of the Holy Spirit, I also give You permission to
do in me and through me whatever You desire, and whatever will glorify
You.**

In Jesus' name I pray. Amen.

Final affirmations

As a final act of faith, make these declarations out loud:

- I affirm that it was for freedom that Christ has set me free. I
  therefore choose to keep standing firm and no longer be subject
  to the yoke of slavery. (Galatians 5:1)
- I affirm that, having begun by the Spirit, I am not going to finish
  through the flesh, but through the transforming power of the
  Spirit of liberty. (Galatians 3:3; 2 Corinthians 3:17–18)
- I affirm that the purpose of the Law was to show me my need of
  Christ but now that faith has come I am no longer under the Law.
  (Galatians 3:24–25)
- I affirm that I am now an unconditionally loved, accepted and
  secure child of God in Christ. (Galatians 3:26; Ephesians 1:5–6)
- I affirm that I am now dead to the Law through the body of Christ
  and that I have been joined to the risen Christ in order to bear
  much fruit for God. (Romans 7:4)

- I affirm that I am a bondslave of Jesus Christ and that my life's purpose is to please Him not others. (Galatians 1:10)
- I affirm that the Lord's Word to me is now, "Grace to you and peace from God our Father and the Lord Jesus Christ". (Galatians 1:3)
- I affirm that God's strength is now made perfect in my weakness and that His grace is sufficient for me. (2 Corinthians 12:9)
- Therefore I affirm that by the grace of God I am what I am and that by His grace I stand. (1 Corinthians 15:10; Romans 5:2). All to the praise of His glorious grace, which He freely bestowed on me in Christ. (Ephesians 1:6)

Concluding declaration

By the authority I have in Christ, I now command every enemy of the Lord Jesus Christ to leave my presence. I commit myself to my Heavenly Father to do His will from this day forward. In Jesus' precious name. Amen.

Concluding prayer

Dear Heavenly Father,

I come to You as Your child, bought out of slavery to sin by the blood of the Lord Jesus Christ. You are the Lord of the universe and the Lord of my life. I submit my body to You as an instrument of righteousness, a living and holy sacrifice that will glorify You. I now ask You to fill me to overflowing with Your Holy Spirit today and every day. I commit myself to the renewing of my mind, in order to prove that Your will is good, pleasing and perfect for me. I choose to live in the grace, peace and rest that are mine in the Lord Jesus Christ.

Amen.

Lies List

After each session, use these two pages to make a list of areas where you realize that your belief system has not been in line with what God says is true in His Word. Record the lie in the left-hand column and, if you can, use the right-hand column to record what is actually true from the Bible. You will have opportunity to address them during *The Steps To Experiencing God's Grace* and also by using Stronghold-Busting (see pages 62–64). Use a separate sheet of paper or notebook if there are too many to fit!

Remember, you are transformed by the renewal of your mind (Romans 12:2). Identifying faulty thinking and replacing it with what is actually true is a crucial part of *The Grace Course*. It takes effort but it's well worth it!

LIE	TRUTH
[Example:] I am dirty	I have been washed clean by the blood of the lamb (Revelation 7:14)
The father loves me but has been let down by me.	The father loves me as much as he loves Jesus John 17v23
	I am protected, held in Jesus and the fathers hands. John 10 27-30
I am facing all problems alone. As a test	I will never be deserted or forsaken by Christ Heb 13v5
I am stuck in sin.	I can walk by the holy spirit instead of giving into the lusts of my flesh Gal 5.16 18:28
I cant do anything right, and my best is not good enough.	The father accepts me in Christ Just as I am. eph 1v6
I must measure up to certain standards in order to be a valuable person	I am the righteousness of God in Christ, therefore in him I do measure up. 2 cor 5:21

I AM A MIGHTY WARRIOR

LIE	TRUTH
God is distant and uninterested in me	My father God is intimate & involved Psm 139 1-18
God is absent or too busy for me.	father God is always with me and eager to be with me.